S Harry A Mullins

ABOUT THE AUTHOR—

KEITH L. BROOKS

Began his career as a newspaperman and publisher . . .

Has been active in the evangelistic
field as a musician and Bible
teacher . . .

Is an outstanding scholar and ex-
ponent of prophecy . . .

Is the president of the American
Prophetic League, Inc. . . .

Is the editor of *Prophecy Monthly,*
the official monthly publication of
the League . . .

Has written scores of pamphlets
and Bible study books, many of
which have been translated into
numerous languages for use on
mission fields . . .

Is the author of *Prophetic Questions Answered, Children's Gospel
Commentary, Riches of Genesis,
Rich Renderings of Holy Writ*
and many other widely-circulated
volumes . . .

ILLUSTRATIONS FOR PREACHERS
AND SPEAKERS

ILLUSTRATIONS FOR PREACHERS AND SPEAKERS

Especially Adapted to
the Quiet Hour

by
KEITH L. BROOKS, D. D.
Editor, *Prophecy Monthly*
Author, *Prophetic Questions Answered, Children's Gospel Commentary,* etc.

ZONDERVAN PUBLISHING HOUSE
GRAND RAPIDS, MICHIGAN

EIGHT FORTY-SEVEN OTTAWA AVENUE
GRAND RAPIDS, MICHIGAN

DEDICATION

To my daughter, Pauline Eleanor Brooks, these devotional stories
are dedicated, since for her benefit they were originally prepared
with Scriptural setting for use in the devotional circle of the
home. When their effectiveness was realized, they were printed
in a little book, *Quiet Hour Stories,* for use in Christian Endeavor
and other young people's groups, and it has been a joy to hear
of spiritual blessings that have resulted in many young lives.
The publishers of this present volume saw in these prayerfully-
chosen anecdotes a wealth of ready material for Christian
speakers in general, and we are glad to have the material go
forth in this more permanent form, for it is certain that the
masses of mankind must be impressed by illustrative teaching
if they are to be impressed at all.

KEITH L. BROOKS

CONTENTS

Contents

TOPICAL INDEX

Topical Index

Topical Index

"THE LIFE WHICH I NOW LIVE"

I am crucified with Christ: nevertheless I live; yet not I, but Christ liveth in me: and the life which I now live in the flesh I live by the faith of the Son of God, who loved me, and gave himself for me (Galatians 2:20).

The life which I now live! What is it? Is it His life within, making ours radiant? Is it His life reproduced by the power of the indwelling Spirit? If so, it will take His faith to make real this supernatural life. It is lived *by the faith of the Son of God.* Mark 11:22 is literally: "Have the faith of God." Faith is taking hold of Him, like taking hold of the handles of a static machine: the power grips you and you cannot let go. I stood by the bedside of an invalid in Erie, Pennsylvania, who had not been out of his room in seventeen years. He had not a dollar of income, yet in answer to his prayers for daily bread, money was found regularly tucked under his door. People, many of them unsaved, flocked to his room requesting his prayers. He had a spiritual influence more far-reaching than many pastors in that city. He amused himself in spare moments by whittling out little emblems such as crosses, anchors, fish, etc., to which were attached fitting Bible verses. On the foot of his bed was a dishpan full of these which visitors might select as mementos. Thinking to bring the sufferer some word of encouragement, I said: "Mr. Anderson, the work you are doing here is wonderful." He held up his thin hand to stop me: "Anderson?" he said: "Anderson has been dead these seventeen years — crucified with Christ. The life I now live is not the old life of Anderson — it is Christ. If anything is accomplished, all praise to Him!" His was indeed a resurrection life in advance.

13

"WE SHALL BE LIKE HIM"

Beloved, now are we the sons of God, and it doth
not yet appear what we shall be: but we know that,
when he shall appear, we shall be like him; for we shall
see him as he is (I John 3:2).

A Danish missionary in India, with the help of a native, was
working on the translation of this chapter. There was a pause
as the helper put down his pen, and sought to find an expression
that would make an acceptable rendering. *"Like Him,"* said the
helper: "that is too much. We will say: 'When He shall appear,
we shall kiss His feet.'" The missionary insisted that God's own
amazing statement must be recorded. What blessings are hung
upon this single event of the future — *"When he shall appear"!*
Dr. Wilbur Chapman sat beside an old soldier in England. The
old fellow related how one of his companions in the Crimean
War had suffered the loss of both legs. The day came when they
were to appear before the queen for their medals. "Someone
pinned one on me," he said, "but when the queen saw the
legless man, lying thin and white on a stretcher, she took his
medal in her own hands and as she bent over him, exclaiming,
'My brave soldier, my brave soldier!' tears fell upon his face. My
friend never mentioned the medal afterward," continued the
veteran," but he would always say: 'Boys, I looked into the face
of the queen: that's reward enough for me!'" What will it mean
for God's children to look into the Saviour's face when He ap-
pears? Transformation complete — reward glorious and eternal!

OUR FRIEND'S UNLIMITED CREDIT

Whatsoever ye shall ask in my name, that will I do,
that the Father may be glorified in the Son. If ye shall
ask any thing in my name, I will do it (John 14:13-14).

Mozart, the great musician, walking one day in the suburbs
of Vienna, was accosted by a beggar who told his tale of woe
with such effect as to interest the great composer in his favor.

But the state of Mozart's purse did not correspond with the impulse of his humanity. He asked his applicant to follow him to a coffee house. Here Mozart, drawing some paper from his pocket, in a few moments composed a minuet, and with a letter he gave it to the distressed man, and desired him to take it to his publisher. A composition from Mozart was a bill payable at sight with his publisher at any time. The happy beggar was immediately given a good sum on handing in the music manuscript. Oh, what an advantage it is to have a Divine Friend who has unlimited credit in heaven and in whose Name we may come at any time to the treasure house when we are in need. *My God shall supply all your need according to his riches in glory by Christ Jesus* (Philippians 4:19). No checks on the bank of heaven, presented in the Name of God's own Son, can be protested for lack of funds. To have His merits and His resources available to us means the covering of every need, not for time, but for all eternity.

THE JOY OF THE REDEEMED

[He] gave HIMSELF for our sins (Galatians 1:4). The Son of man came . . . to give his life a ransom for many (Matthew 20:28). [He] hath given HIMSELF for us an offering and a sacrifice to God for a sweetsmelling savour (Ephesians 5:2).

Many years ago the tears of a slave girl about to be sold drew the attention of a man as he passed through the slave mart in a Southern state. The kind man stopped to ask why she wept, when others who were being auctioned appeared indifferent. She had been reared with much care by a kind owner and was terrified to think who might buy her. The man asked her price. He hesitated when he learned the amount, but finally paid it. Yet no joy seemed to come to the slave's face when he told her she was free. She had been born a slave and knew not what freedom meant. Her tears fell fast on the signed parchment which her deliverer brought to her to prove to her that now she was free. Finally she realized what freedom was. With her first breath she exclaimed: "I will follow him. I must serve him all my life." To every reason given her against it by her friends, she only cried: "He redeemed me! He redeemed me!" She insisted on going to his home to work. When strangers visited that home and noticed how devoted and faithful was her service, she had but one answer: "He redeemed me! He redeemed me!" Oh, that we could realize the full meaning of the fact that the Lord of Glory has redeemed us! Should not our hearts be thrilled to realize that we are no longer in bondage to Satan and doomed to a place of eternal suffering? Let us serve Him as sinners bought back with precious blood.

AWAKENING IN HIS PRESENCE

Jesus said . . . I am the resurrection, and the life: he that believeth in me, though he were dead, yet shall he live: and whosoever liveth and believeth in me shall never die. Believest thou this? (John 11:25-26). For we know that if our earthly house of this tabernacle were dissolved, we have a building of God, an house not made with hands, eternal in the heavens (II Corinthians 5:1).

Ian Maclaren often related a story which served to allay the needless fears of God's people when they enter the valley of the shadow of death. There was a dear old Scotch lady who wanted badly to go to the city of Edinburgh, but for years she could not be persuaded to take the railway journey because of her great dread of a tunnel through which she would have to pass. One day circumstances arose which compelled her to go. For a while her fears were great and her agitation increased as the train drew near the dreaded tunnel. But before the tunnel was actually reached the old lady, worn out with excitement, dropped peacefully off to sleep. When she awoke she discovered that the tunnel had been passed. The resurrection hope in Christ

takes the sting out of death. *Though I walk through the valley
. . . of death, I will fear no evil: for thou art with me.* We shall
awake in the full sunshine of His presence.

THE FELLOWSHIP OF SAINTS

> That which we have seen and heard declare we
> unto you, that ye also may have fellowship with us:
> and truly our fellowship is with the Father, and with
> his Son Jesus Christ . . . If we walk in the light, as he
> is in the light, we have fellowship one with another,
> and the blood of Jesus Christ his Son cleanseth us from
> all sin (I John 1:3, 7).

The happy and blessed life cannot be lived in separation
from others of God's family. More and more, as the age rushes
toward its consummation, we need the communion of the saints;
therefore, we are bidden not to forsake the assembling of ourselves together, *and so much the more, as ye see the day ap-
proaching* (Hebrews 10:25). Where can one find in this world
such fellowship as that which exists among God's true children?
Dr. George A. Buttrick, a well-known minister, was vacationing in
Michigan. An ardent trout fisherman, he was fishing up a new
stream in the afternoon. As he waded around a bend, there came
the sound of the singing of old hymns. He crossed the stream
and found a barn whence came the singing. He went in and
found farm people sitting on rude benches facing a leader and
singing with heart and soul. Between songs simple testimonies
were given. After a while the leader turned to the stranger and
asked if he had a word for the Lord. "And there," said Dr.
Buttrick, "in that old barn, surrounded by humble folk, with a
rod in one hand and a creel over my shoulder, I rejoiced in the
fellowship of saints as I tried to add my word to the story of
Jesus and His love."

THE LORD — OUR HELPER

Let your [manner of life] be without covetousness; and be content with such things as ye have: for he hath said, I will never leave thee, nor forsake thee. So that we may boldly say, The Lord is my helper, and I will not fear what man shall do unto me (Hebrews 13:5-6).

At one time Bishop Gabot of Jerusalem was greatly discouraged when making a missionary journey in Abyssinia. All seemed against him and he felt God had forsaken him. He found a cave and went into it, spending a long time in prayer, telling the Lord how forsaken he was. It was very dark in the cave but after he had remained in the dark for some time, his eyes became accustomed to it and he saw there a ferocious wild animal, a hyena and her cubs. God had protected him and the animals had made no move to touch him. God's hand at that very hour when Bishop Gabot thought He was against him, was keeping him from being torn to pieces, for there is no animal more ferocious than a hyena with her cubs. He escaped unharmed. If we would but permit God to open our eyes in the darkness when it seems we are forsaken, we would see that He is ever mindful of us, keeping us from many unseen dangers and calamities. In the very hour of our greatest despair we may find we have greatest reason to thank Him. If circumstances find us in God, we will always find God in our circumstances.

"THE MORNING COMETH"

Watchman, what of the night? Watchman, what of the night? The watchman said, The morning cometh, and also the night (Isaiah 21:11-12).

A call came to the prophet of Seir: *Watchman, what of the night?* God's people everywhere are today longing to know what remains of the night of this age. Are there any signs of the dawn of a better day? Will the Bridegroom soon be here? Yes, many see light on the hills. Those who study prophecy cannot fail to sense the nearness of our Lord's Second Coming, when He shall appear as *the Sun of righteousness.* "One little hour — and then the glorious crowning, the golden harp strings and the victor's palm! One little hour and then the hallelujah, eternity's long, deep, thanksgiving psalm!" Years ago a maiden's lover went away on an expedition to the Holy Land after promising to return to take his bride. Months went by without word, and reports came back that the lover had perished, but the maiden refused to believe all such reports. Night after night, year after year, she kept a light in the window, believing that sometime his bark would be guided to the shore of her island home. Her hope was not disappointed, for one night her lover returned after years during which he had been stranded on a lonely isle. Let the story be to us a parable of the Church waiting the return of her Lover, now in heaven. Some argue that it is foolish to expect His return. The light in the window is the flame of hope that ever symbolizes His return. Nothing else can end the night of sorrow and sin. "Yet a little while, how short, how short. The coming one will be here and will not delay" (Hebrews 10: 31, Rotherham).

SUFFERING AND SERVICE

Being justified by faith, we have peace with God through our Lord Jesus Christ: by whom also we have access by faith into his grace wherein we stand, and rejoice in hope of the glory of God. And not only so, but we glory in tribulations also: knowing that tribulation worketh patience; and patience, experience; and experience, hope (Romans 5:1-4).

Tribulation and misfortune have created many geniuses, even apart from Christian faith. Demosthenes stuttered and applied himself so rigidly that he became a great orator. The liberal and wise Alfred the Great was a lifelong victim of internal disease. Carlyle was a dispeptic. Some of the greatest stories of achievement concern sufferers who found hope and courage in Christ. Milton was blind. The creative genius of Elizabeth Browning was expressed in the few years when the ravages of tuberculosis were worst. William Cowper, Isaac Newton, Coleridge and Poe were victims, at times, of insanity. The genius of Beethoven expressed itself most forcibly when he began to lose his hearing and his work attained sublimity when he became totally deaf. Normal health and normal bodies would have robbed us of many of the world's most outstanding characters. Tremendous drive marks a true genius. Often it is begun in the effort to surmount limitations, and when the Holy Spirit becomes the empowering agent, fruitage is far-reaching and eternal in results.

GOD REMEMBERS

> The law of the Lord is perfect, converting the soul: the testimony of the Lord is sure, making wise the simple. The statutes of the Lord are right, rejoicing the heart . . . More to be desired are they than gold, yea, than much fine gold: sweeter also than honey and the honeycomb . . . In keeping of them there is great reward (Psalm 19:7-11).

When Dr. W. P. White was in his first pastorate he was called to see a dying member of the church, one of the most godly men in the congregation. The young minister wondered what he, in his inexperience, could say to such a saint of God. He prayed much that God would give him words that would help the sufferer. When he reached the home he found the man in tears. "For years," said the man, "I have been memorizing the precious promises of the Word of God. I thought when I came to my last hours I could repeat them all and find great comfort in them, but now my memory has failed me completely and I can recall only snatches of a few of them." Dr. White prayed for wisdom, then, quick as a flash, the answer came. "Do you think God has forgotten them?" he asked the sufferer. "No, of course He hasn't forgotten," answered the man. "Then, why not just rest in the *Promiser Himself?*" was his advice. In that answer the dying man found joy and he fell into a peaceful sleep from which he did not awake in this world. We can rest in the remembrance of God, even when our memories fail us.

LIVING EPISTLES

Bear ye one another's burdens, and so fulfil the
law of Christ . . . Let us not be weary in well doing: for
in due season we shall reap, if we faint not. As we
have therefore opportunity, let us do good unto all men,
especially unto them who are of the household of faith
(Galatians 6:2, 9-10).

Dr. Cortland Myers boarded a train enroute to a city where
he was to speak. He hoped to prepare his messages while on the
train. He spread out his books over two seats and began his
studying. A fat lady and four dirty children were seated behind
him. One boy started climbing on the back of Dr. Myers' seat and
putting dirty fingers on his collar. He was minded to put the
boy in his place. Instead, Dr. Myers bought some candy for all the
children. Hours went by and he was unable to work on his
sermons, but instead, spent his time telling stories to the urchins.
A man about to leave the train came to Dr. Myers and, with
tears in his eyes, thanked him for his kindness to these children.
He said the people in the car had been watching and saying:
"That's real Christianity." "I do not understand," said Dr.
Myers. He was told that the old lady was the grandmother. The
mother was in a coffin in the baggage car. "Be careful how you
travel," was Dr. Myer's advice. "Remember that others are watching to see if your Christianity is all talk!"

THE ONE WAY IN

All have sinned, and come short of the glory of
God; being justified freely by his grace through the re-
demption that is in Christ Jesus: whom God hath set
forth to be a propitiation through faith in his blood,
to declare his righteousness for the remission of sins
that are past, through the forbearance of God (Romans
3:23-25).

Dr. Charles Barry, a liberal preacher of England, was pre-
paring for bed one night when a poor woman came to his door

saying: "My mother is dying. I want you to come and get her in!" The minister understood that the dying woman wanted peace in her heart so that she could face her Maker. He consented to go, wondering how he could adapt his ideas of the Gospel to a sinful, dying soul. He talked to the gasping woman about the advantage of having a good record. He told her there was no reason to fear anything since God is love and all is God. He told her to blot out the past and throw herself on the mercy of God. But none of this brought rest to the sin-sick soul. The minister became desperate. He well knew what this woman was waiting to hear. He could think only of the hymn he often heard his mother sing when he was a lad. He began to sing: "There is a fountain filled with blood — "

Seeing that a light came into the woman's face, the minister recalled as best he could the story of the Lamb of God crucified in the sinner's place, as it had been taught him in his early days. The dying woman was given faith in that moment to receive Jesus as her Saviour and Redeemer. *He got her in!* But Dr. Barry did something more. When the next Sunday morning he told the story to his fashionable congregation, he added: "And it got me in, too!"

THE WISER WAY

> I say unto you which hear, Love your enemies, do good to them which hate you, bless them that curse you, and pray for them which despitefully use you (Luke 6:27-28).

A poor widow who made her living by taking in washings depended greatly upon produce from her garden. One night several boys robbed her garden and, to make matters worse, turned some pigs into the garden so that it was ruined by morning. The widow had to suffer through the winter because of the loss of her vegetables. As she looked at the ruined garden she picked up a knife with a name engraved on the handle. It was the name of a boy she knew. However, nothing was said about the matter.

During the ensuing months a revival took place in the town and among those who became convicted of sin was the owner of the knife. He was converted and obeyed his conscience when it told him he must go to the widow and confess his part in what had been done. She told him she had long known of his act and showed him the knife. "Why didn't you report me and make me pay the damage?" he asked. "There was a more excellent way," she said. "I began to pray that God would save your soul, then I knew you would want to make everything right. I knew, too, that God would supply my need and above all, that He would give me the joy of seeing a soul saved." The boy learned that day something of what the Holy Spirit is able to put into the hearts of God's true children.

HEIRS OF GOD

> The Spirit itself beareth witness with our spirit, that we are the children of God: and if children, then heirs; heirs of God, and joint-heirs with Christ; if so be that we suffer with him, that we may be also glorified together (Romans 8:16-17). According to his abundant mercy [he] hath begotten us again unto a lively hope . . . to an inheritance incorruptible, and undefiled, and that fadeth not away, reserved in heaven for you (I Peter 1:3-4).

A rich man's wife died. Not long afterward their only child, a little boy whom both dearly loved, followed his mother to the grave. The man never recovered from the shock of the double bereavement. After his death, search was made for a will but none was found. At the sale of the house and furniture, an old servant of the household was present, wanting to buy a portrait of the lad whom she loved much. She purchased the painting and when it was taken down from the wall, a will was found fastened to the back of it. When it was read it was discovered that the person who, at the sale of the effects, should purchase the picture of the much-loved son, should be heir to all the property. Yes, and God said to those who love His only begotten Son and are willing to suffer for Him, that He will make them heirs of His eternal kingdom. All depends upon our relationship to His beloved Son. To know and love Him is to share with Him in riches incorruptible and everlasting.

"NONE OTHER NAME"

Neither is there salvation in any other: for there is none other name under h e a v e n given among men, whereby we must be saved (Acts 4:12). Jesus saith . . . I am the way, the truth, and the life: no man cometh unto the Father, but by me (John 14:6).

A few persons were standing near a blind man who had taken his station on a bridge in a certain city. He was reading aloud from his Braille Bible. A man on his way home, led by curiosity, stopped at the edge of the crowd. Just then the blind man was reading at Acts 4:12 and lost his place. While trying to find it with his finger, he constantly repeated the last clause he had read: *None other name, none other name.* Some smiled at his embarrassment, but the man at the edge of the crowd walked away deeply musing. He had lately been under conviction for sin. He had been seeking in many ways to find peace. Religious exercises, good resolutions and altered habits did not enable him to rejoice in the Lord. Ringing in his ears were the words: *None other name, none other name!* When he retired at night these words kept chiming in his mind. *None other name!* At last the music entered his soul. "I see it," he said. "I have been trying to find peace through my own works, my reformation, my prayers. It is Jesus alone who can save. Lord, I receive You as my Saviour!" That moment the joy of salvation flooded his heart.

IMPORTANT BUSINESS

They that be wise shall shine as the brightness of the firmament; and they that turn many to righteousness as the stars for ever and ever (Daniel 12:3). To the weak became I as weak, that I might gain the weak: I

am made all things to all men, that I might by all means
save some (I Corinthians 9:22).

Gladstone, the great English statesman, when he was at the
height of his popularity, one day noticed that an old man who
used to sweep street crossings for gratuitous pennies near the
House of Parliament was no longer there. He learned that the man
was ill. He obtained his address, and, leaving his busy place in
the House of Parliament, he found his way down a dirty lonely
alley and into a hovel where the man lay. Sitting on a common
stool beside the ragged bed, Gladstone took his Testament from
his pocket and after reading salvation passages, knelt and prayed
for the man. Later a missionary called to see the old man. "You
must be very lonely in such a place with no one to comfort you,"
he said. "No," was the unexpected reply. "Mr. Gladstone came
here and left behind him Jesus, the Saviour. I took Him as my
Lord and now I do not feel alone." Most of us think we are
too busy to make such calls, but this great man who carried
tremendous responsibilities felt he had no appointment more important than witnessing of Christ to a needy soul. Perhaps there
are those of our own flesh and blood to whom we have never
spoken about Christ.

TASTE OF HEAVEN

To do good and to [be liberal] forget not: for with
such sacrifices God is well pleased (Hebrews 13:16). Dis-
tributing to the necessity of saints; given to hospitality
(Romans 12:13). Let us not love [simply] in word,
neither in tongue; but in deed and in truth (I John
3:18).

"Pastor," a church member once said to the minister, "that
was a wonderful sermon you preached on heaven Sunday
morning, but you did not tell us where heaven is." "Ah," said
the pastor, "I cannot tell you its exact location but I can tell
you how you can get a taste of it in advance." "How is that?"
asked the man. "Over yonder on that hill," said the pastor, "lies

a member of our church who lies in bed week after week. Her two children are now sick and also in bed. They have little food in the house, they need warm blankets and there is no one to split wood to warm their home. You go up there and take a few things with you, and say: 'Sister, I have brought these in our Saviour's Name,' and do what you can to help; then, before you leave, take your Bible and read to them and get down and pray — and if you do not find heaven before you are through, I will pay the bill." The next day the same man met the pastor again. "I've had a little of heaven," he exclaimed. "I spent a half-hour in heaven yesterday." Heaven begins here below for those who render loving service in the Master's Name.

THE STARTING PLACE

Who can find a virtuous woman? for her price is far above rubies. The heart of her husband doth safely trust in her . . . She openeth her mouth with wisdom; and in her tongue is the law of kindness. She looketh well to the ways of her household . . . Her children arise up, and call her blessed; her husband also, and he praiseth her . . . A woman that feareth the Lord, she shall be praised (Proverbs 31:10, 11, 26, 27, 28, 30).

One day Henry W. Grady, the great newspaperman, left his editorial room and went to his old home to see his mother. He was confused religiously. His first words to his mother were: "Mother, I've lost my religion and I've come back to you where I first found God, that you might lead me to Him again." She bade him sit beside her as she told him the story of Jesus and His love and His great sacrifice upon the Cross. She sang to him the lullabies she had sung in his childhood. She gave him bread and milk at the table, as when he was a boy. She led him to bed and as she finally tucked him in, she said: "Let's pray our little prayer, 'Now I lay me down to sleep.'" In the morning when Mr. Grady came down to breakfast, he said: "It's all right, Mother. I'm back to God again. I feel as I did in my childhood."

With great joy he went to his office to work. There are many who have wandered away from Mother's Bible and Mother's Christ. Let us go back to the starting place.

THE LAMB OF GOD

> John seeth Jesus coming unto him, and saith, Behold the Lamb of God, which taketh away the sin of the world (John 1:29). All we like sheep have gone astray; we have turned every one to his own way; and the Lord hath laid on him the iniquity of us all (Isaiah 53:6).

There is an old but true story of a man who was traveling in Norway. He went to see a church in a certain town. As he looked up at the tower, he saw the carved figure of a lamb near the top. He asked why it had been placed in this position and was told the following incident. One day, when the church was being built, a workman fell from the high scaffold about the tower. The men working with him saw him fall and were transfixed with fear. They reached the ground as quickly as possible, expecting to find the body dashed to pieces, but to their surprise, he was virtually unhurt. A flock of sheep were being driven past the church at the moment of his fall. He had fallen on one of the lambs. The lamb was crushed to death, but the man was saved. The carved figure of a lamb was placed on the tower not only to commemorate the event but to remind all of the Son of God who came into this world to die as the Lamb of God in the place of every sinner who would receive Him. *He was wounded for our transgressions, he was bruised for our iniquities* (Isaiah 53:5).

THE ROSE OF SHARON

> We are unto God a sweet savour of Christ, in them that are saved, and in them that perish (II Corinthians 2:15). Thanks be unto God who always leadeth us forth to triumph in the beloved one, and who diffuseth by us the fragrance of the knowledge of him in every place (v. 14-free trans.).

Dr. Campbell Morgan relates that he once went into the home of a man who was entertaining him, and in one room he had always detected a strong fragrance of roses. He said to his host one day: "I wish you would tell me why, whenever I come into this room, I smell the fragrance of roses." The gentleman smiled and replied: "Ten years ago I was in the Holy Land, and while there I bought a small tube of attar of roses. It was wrapped in cotton wool, and as I was standing here unpacking it, suddenly I broke the bottle. I put the broken container, cotton wool and all, into the vase on the mantel." There stood a beautiful vase, and he lifted the lid and the fragrance of roses filled the room. That fragrance had permeated the clay of the vase and it was impossible for one to enter the room without being conscious of it. Dr. Morgan often used the incident as an illustration of the fact that if Christ be given pre-eminence in the life of the Christian, the fragrance of the Rose of Sharon will pervade and permeate the entire life, making others conscious of the presence of One whom they do not see.

A MESSAGE OF CONTRASTS

Jesus said . . . I am the resurrection, and the life (John 11:25). In a moment, in the twinkling of an eye, at the last trump . . . the dead shall be raised incorruptible, and we shall be changed. For this corruptible must put on incorruption, and this mortal must put on immortality (I Corinthians 15:52-53).

Dr. Jowett relates that two months before the First World War he was in a hamlet 4,000 feet among the Alps. He lifted his eyes from the paper on which he had written the words, *I am the resurrection, and the life.* When he gazed upon the mountain with its mantle of freshly fallen snow, glistening brilliantly in the morning light, he heard the roar of falling waters, much louder after the previous day's rain. Birds were singing blithely. Scents were rising from the meadows like incense from a great altar. "I turned my eyes away from the mountain," he said, "and

looked at a house up the road. The blinds were drawn. Death
had paid a visit in the night. Flowers were withering in the
yard by the house. I recalled the words: *As a flower of the field,
so he flourisheth; for the wind passeth over it and it is gone;
and the place thereof shall know it no more.* Then I looked at
my notebook and the words *I am the resurrection, and the life!*
What a glad message of contrast! Thank God, if there is a power
that maketh for death, there is also a power that maketh for
life! The body may be sown in weakness, but it will be raised
in power. It may be sown in dishonor, but it will be raised in
glory (I Corinthians 15:43)."

UP FROM THE DEPTHS

> **He brought me up also out of an horrible pit, out
> of the miry clay, and set my feet upon a rock, and estab-
> lished my goings. And he hath put a new song in my
> mouth, even praise unto our God: many shall see it, and
> fear, and shall trust in the Lord (Psalm 40:2-3). Christ
> Jesus came into the world to save sinners; of whom I am
> chief (I Timothy 1:15).**

John Newton, who ran away to sea and then to Africa, was
sold at last to a negress. He sank so low that he lived on crumbs
from her table and on wild yams dug at night. His clothing was
reduced to a single shirt which he washed in the ocean. When
he finally escaped, he lived the base life of the natives. It does
not seem possible for a civilized man to have sunk so low. But
the power of Jesus laid hold of him through a missionary. He
became a sea captain, and later, a minister. He wrote many hymns
sung the world around — "Safely Through Another Week,"
"Come, My Soul," "Glorious Things of Thee Are Spoken," "How
Sweet the Name of Jesus Sounds," and "One There Is Above All
Others." In the Church of London, of which he was the pastor,
there is still an epitaph John Newton wrote for himself. It reads:
"Sacred to the memory of John Newton, once a libertine and
blasphemer and slave of slaves in Africa, but renewed, purified,

pardoned and appointed to preach that Gospel which he labored to destroy." The influence of that life, once so low in sin, through the grace of God, will go on to bless thousands everywhere until Jesus comes again.

SAFE AMIDST CHAOS

> There shall be . . . upon the earth distress of nations, with perplexity; the sea and the waves roaring; men's hearts failing them for fear, and for looking after those things which are coming on the earth . . . And then shall they see the Son of man coming in a cloud with power and great glory. And when these things begin to come to pass, then look up, and lift up your heads; for your redemption draweth nigh (Luke 21: 25-28).

During a frightful storm in the Georgian Bay of Canada years ago, a ship was wrecked. Many perished. The mate, with six strong men and one timid girl, escaped in a boat but the waves were high and the craft turned over and over until, one by one, the strong men lost their hold and disappeared beneath the angry billows. The mate, however, lashed the girl to the prow of the boat, and thus she drifted to the shore, where she was found by an Indian. She lived many years after the experience. She did not escape by her skill or wisdom — only because she was fastened firmly to that which could not sink. When the stalwart men went down with shrieks of despair, she was saved through the thoughtfulness that lashed her to the lifeboat. A storm is fast gathering over the world and the Church, as long ago foretold by our Lord. Multitudes are being swept away in sin and apostasy to go down forever in darkness and death. There is hope today only for those who are lashed to the sure promises of God's Word *which liveth and abideth for ever.*

A HEAVENLY CALLING

Holy brethren, partakers of the heavenly calling, consider [lit. "think again and again"] the Apostle and High Priest of our profession, Christ Jesus (Hebrews 3:1. Preach the word; be instant in season, out of season; reprove, rebuke, exhort with all longsuffering and doctrine (II Timothy 4:2).

Dr. Bob Jones, the president of Bob Jones College, was on a speaking tour in Alabama. He had to drive to Birmingham to have his car overhauled, but on the morning of his departure, rain was falling in torrents. He started nevertheless, after prayer, on the muddy roads. Ten miles in the country the car slipped into a ditch. Dr. Jones had felt certain that God had led him to start. In pouring rain and mud he walked to a small farmhouse. His knock was answered by a call, "Come in." There sat a man with a group of little children around him. He was trying to dress one little fellow. Dr. Jones asked if the man could get a mule and help pull his car out of the mud. The man looked up, tears running down his face. "I'll help," he said, "as soon as I can dress these children. I buried their mother yesterday." Dr. Jones took one little girl on his lap and put on her ragged stockings, helping with others, as he told the father of the Lord Jesus. "I ought to be a Christian," said the man. "My wife talked to me a lot about it, and I have these kiddies to raise." Putting his arm around him, Dr. Jones said: "We'll settle that right now!" He left the house, thanking God for the heavenly calling that directed him in strange ways to this needy family, for he left them all rejoicing in the Lord. Is there any work more blessed than witnessing for Christ?

THE LIVING LORD

[They] . . . came to see the sepulchre . . . The angel of the Lord . . . came and rolled back the stone from the door, and sat upon it . . . The angel . . . said unto the women . . . I know that ye seek Jesus, which

was crucified. He is not here: for he is risen, as he said.
Come, see the place where the Lord lay (Matthew
28:1-6). I am he that liveth, and was dead; and, behold,
I am alive for evermore (Revelation 1:18).

Dr. Dale was once writing an Easter sermon. When he was
half through, the thought of the risen Lord broke in upon him
as it had never done before. "Christ is alive!" he said to himself
— *alive for evermore!* He paused and repeated: "He is *alive* this
very minute, living as certainly as I myself am." He arose,
repeating as he walked, "Christ is *living!*" At first it seemed
strange and hardly true, and then it came to him as a sudden
burst of glory — Christ is now living! It was like a new discovery
although he thought he had believed it before. Then he said: "I
must get this across to my people. I shall preach about it again
and again until they realize it as I do now." For months after, and
in every sermon, the *living Christ* was his one great theme, and
there and then began the custom of singing in that great church
an Easter hymn on every Sunday morning. Have we laid hold
of the fact that we have a *living* Lord, One who *ever liveth
to make intercession for* [us], and to act for us in every time of
need?

THE SECRET OF POWER

He that goeth forth and weepeth, bearing precious
seed, shall doubtless come again with rejoicing, bringing
his sheaves with him (Psalm 126:6). Though I speak
with the tongues of men and of angels, and have not
[love], I am become as sounding brass, or a tinkling
cymbal (I Corinthians 13:1).

Dr. Cortland Myers in his book *How Do We Know?* tells of
Robert Murray McCheyne, one of Scotland's greatest preachers,
who died at the age of twenty-nine. Everywhere he stepped,
Scotland shook. Whenever he opened his mouth a spiritual force
swept in every direction. Thousands followed him into God's
kingdom. A traveler, eager to see where McCheyne had preached,
went to the Scotch town and found the church. An old gray-

haired sexton agreed to take him through the church. He led the way into McCheyne's study. "Sit in that chair," he ordered. The traveler hesitated a moment, then sat down. On the table before him was an open Bible. "Drop your head on that Book and weep. That is the way our minister always did before he preached," said the old man. He then led the visitor into the pulpit before the open Bible. "Stand there," he said, "and drop your head on your hands and let the tears flow. That is the way our minister always did before he began to preach!" With such a passion for lost and needy souls, is it any wonder that the Holy Spirit gave McCheyne a magnetic personality which drew many into the family of God?

BURY YOUR SORROW

Wherein ye greatly rejoice, though now for a season, if need be, ye are in heaviness through manifold [testings]: that the trial of your faith, being much more precious than of gold that perisheth, though it be tried with fire, might be found unto praise and honour and glory at the appearing of Jesus Christ (I Peter 1:6-7).

One of the beautiful hymns, "Go Bury Thy Sorrow," came out of the experience of Mary Bachelor. She was a minister's daughter and acted as a housekeeper and helper to her brother, also a minister. She had fallen into the habit of constantly complaining about her trials and sorrows. She regularly unloaded all her burdens upon her brother until one day she noticed deep lines of care written upon his countenance, due to the many burdens he himself had to carry. She looked out of the window and saw the tall poplar trees cast deep shadows in the setting sun. "I am like those to my brother," she thought, "always casting shadows! Why don't I bury my troubles?" She went up to her bedroom and found relief in tears and prayer, after which she wrote the lines:

Go bury thy sorrow,
  The world hath its share;
Go bury it deeply,
  Go hide it with care.
Go think of it calmly
  When curtained by night;
Go tell it to Jesus,
  And all will be right.
Go gather the sunshine
  He sheds on the way;
He'll lighten thy burden —
  Go, weary one, pray.

THE POWER OF CHOICE

If it seem evil unto you to serve the Lord, choose
you this day whom ye will serve . . . but as for me and
my house, we will serve the Lord (Joshua 24:15). Ho,
every one that thirsteth, come ye to the waters, and he
that hath no money; come ye . . . Wherefore do ye
spend money for that which is not bread? and your
labour for that which satisfieth not? hearken diligently
unto me, and eat ye that which is good, and let your
soul delight itself in fatness (Isaiah 55:1-2).

On the day in 1874 that David Livingstone, the great missionary to Africa, was buried in Westminster Abbey, the streets
of London were lined with thousands seeking to pay respect to the
memory of the great pioneer. In the crowd was a poor old man,
unkempt, poorly clad, weeping bitterly. Someone asked him why
he was weeping when all were seeking to honor the illustrious
dead. "I'll tell you why," the old man replied. "David Livingstone
and I were born in the same village, brought up in the same
school and Sunday school, worked together in the same room.
But Davie went *that* way and I went *this*. Now he is honored
by the nation and Christians everywhere, but I am neglected,
unknown and dishonored. I have nothing to look forward to but
a drunkard's grave." The same choice comes to each one, and

that choice determines one's course of life in time, as well as his destiny in eternity. *Seek ye the Lord while he may be found, call ye upon him while he is near* (Isaiah 55:6).

PRAYER IN HIS WILL

This is the confidence that we have in him, that, if we ask any thing according to his will, he heareth us: and if we know that he hear us, whatsoever we ask, we know that we have the petitions that we desired of him (I John 5:14-15).

Much praying is on too low a level. It is in the realm of trivial things, and is, therefore, fleshly and selfish. We can know how to pray according to God's will so that we may come with holy boldness expecting the very thing for which we ask. This is prayer *in the Spirit* (Judges 20; Romans 8:26; Ephesians 6:18). Mrs. Suppes, a widow who lives in Glendale, California, owns and operates some thirty-five rest homes for missionaries. Some years ago this need was laid on her heart and she was led to ask God for $50,000 with which to erect cottages. She had nothing, but her heart was filled with a burning faith. She was confident that $50,000 would be in her hands and immediately opened her little home to take in missionaries. Meanwhile she continued to pray for $50,000. One day a man called and told her a lot she owned was oil land. His company wanted to sink a well and pay her royalties. A gusher of five thousand barrels a day came in. Money began to come into her hands. Missionary homes were erected. She received $50,000 when suddenly the well sanded in. Nothing but salt water could be raised thereafter. God knew the exact amount of oil in that ground. Many more thousands have since come to Mrs. Suppes in answer to prayer and "Mission Road" is known to hundreds of missionaries.

THE FAMILY ALTAR

These words, which I command thee . . . shall be in thine heart: and thou shalt teach them diligently unto thy children, and shalt talk of them when thou sittest in

thine house, and when thou walkest by the way, and
when thou liest down, and when thou risest up. And
thou shalt bind them for a sign upon thine hand . . .
And thou shalt write them upon the posts of thy house
(Deuteronomy 6:6-9).

Thomas Boston was a great minister who spent the early
years of his ministry among the poor of the slums. He found
that the church was cold and empty; he had little influence
through the regular work of the church and was wholly discouraged. Finally he realized that the only way to save the church
is to save the family. He went through the community laboring
to establish family altars and teaching the people how to worship. He visited hundreds of homes and spent three full years in
doing it. Then Dr. Boston's church began to revive, and the
entire community was filled with spiritual power and influence.
Richard Baxter, England's great minister, was another who
spent much of his time in visiting homes and establishing family
worship. He found that family altars furnished a fountainhead
that filled his church to overflowing and started his magnificent
ministry. John G. Paton, the heroic missionary, testified that it
was family worship that started his missionary life and work.

SHINE AS LIGHTS

Ye are the light of the world. A city that is set on
an hill cannot be hid. Let your light so shine before men,
that they may see your good works, and glorify your
Father which is in heaven (Matthew 5:14, 16). That
ye may be blameless and harmless, the sons of God,
without rebuke, in the midst of a crooked and per-
verse nation, among whom ye shine as lights in the
world (Philippians 2:15).

A lighthouse-keeper along the Maine coast one afternoon
left in his rowboat for a near-by village. Soon after, a terrific
storm arose so that it was impossible for him to return. As darkness gathered, his little daughter said to her smaller brother:
"It's getting so dark, and Papa is away. I'll have to light the lamp,

for if I don't, somebody may get lost in the dark." "But you can't light it," replied the lad, "because you can't reach it." She carried a chair up the long winding stairs to the light tower. When she reached the top she found that, even though she stood on the chair, the light switch was far beyond her reach. She went back down and secured a kerosene lamp, and, by standing on tiptoe on the chair, was barely able to reach the huge reflector. There she stood, sending her small bright light across the dark waters until her father returned. The black night of sin has darkened the world. Weary mariners on life's stormy sea will be lost unless we let our lights shine to guide them. Ours may not be a powerful light, but any light is better than none when all is blackness.

THE BLESSED MAN

> Blessed is the man that walketh not in the counsel of the ungodly, nor standeth in the way of sinners, nor sitteth in the seat of the scornful. But his delight is in the law of the Lord; and in his law doth he meditate day and night. And he shall be like a tree planted by the rivers of water, that bringeth forth his fruit in his season . . . and whatsoever he doeth shall prosper (Psalm 1:1-3).

Dr. Myers tells of two men who lived in a country home in their boyhood. They became rich when they left home, but occasionally they visited their old father. Finally, the father went to heaven. The sons did not know what to do with the old house. One said: "You sell your interest to me and I'll tear down the house and build a summer home and you can come out whenever you desire." They made plans to do this and went out together to inspect the house. They stood together beside the old fireplace in silence. Said one: "I've changed my mind. I can't tear down this house." "Strange," said the other, "all I can see is Dad's old chair by the fireplace where he often sat and read his Bible and where we had family prayers when we were young." For two hours they sat by the fireplace and talked; then they knelt together and, with streaming tears, gave their hearts to Christ. The old house had to stand. It was too sacred to sacrifice. It was a spiritual treat for them to spend vacations in the old home where they could think of Father and his Bible.

THE ALL-POWERFUL NAME

> Neither is there salvation in any other: for there is none other name under heaven given among men, whereby we must be saved (Acts 4:12). Thou shalt call his name JESUS: for he shall save his people from their sins (Matthew 1:21). His name shall endure for ever . . . men shall be blessed in him: all nations shall call him blessed (Psalm 72:17).

A middle-aged man arose in a prayer meeting in Boston and said, "I have been thoughtless and sinful until of late. One Sunday evening I was lying on the sofa. My wife had gone out. No one was home but little Mabel, our niece. She began to caress me and said: 'Uncle, tell me something about Jesus. Mamma always does Sunday nights.' I tried to evade it but she would not be put off. I could tell her nothing. Opening her blue eyes wide, she said: 'Why, you *know* about Jesus, don't you?' That question awakened strange feelings. I could not sleep that night. I kept hearing the child's words: 'You *know* about Jesus, don't you?' A sense of ignorance and guilt weighed heavily upon my soul. I read my Bible with an anxious and inquiring heart. At length I found my blessed Saviour and knew I was born again. Now I can say I *know* about Jesus." This life was totally and blessedly changed through the power of one name. Has any other name wrought such transformations in human life? No, this is the *name which is above every name*, the name of the incarnate Son of God who came to redeem us from our sins.

"THANKSGIVING CORNER"

> Let them that suffer according to the will of God commit the keeping of their souls to him in well doing, as unto a faithful Creator (I Peter 4:19). The sufferings of this present time are not worthy to be compared with the glory which shall be revealed in us (Romans 8:18).

In August, 1940, word was received of the home-going of Miss M. R. Higgins, world-famous Christian invalid of Australia, from whose small home, known everywhere as "Thanksgiving Corner," thousands of comforting messages had gone forth to sufferers everywhere for many years. If anyone ever proved the all-sufficiency of divine grace, it was this dear woman who carried on so bravely amid terrible suffering. For fifty years her body was wracked with pain. For forty years she was confined to her bed with both arms gone. She was eighty-three when death came. Her dread malady was "Whitlow disease," but other diseases also afflicted her. It was necessary to extract her finger nails. The skin of her right arm and hand had to be peeled off to check the spread of disease. Both arms finally were removed at the shoulder. Her left leg was also taken. She lost her voice and was blind for long periods. With a special device fitted on her shoulder she penned hundreds of beautiful letters, every stroke necessitating the movement of her whole body and causing severe pain. Hundreds who received her messages were saved and blessed. Who shall say it was not appointed unto her to suffer and glorify Him?

HAPPY DAY

> The Lord is the portion of mine inheritance and of my cup: thou maintainest my lot . . . I will bless the Lord, who hath given me counsel . . . I have set the Lord always before me: because he is at my right hand, I shall not be moved . . . Thou wilt shew me the path

of life: in thy presence is fulness of joy; at thy right
hand there are pleasures for evermore (Psalm 16:
5, 7, 8, 11).

Dr. Panin often told of an old man who made his home
for years in a room on the top floor of a Brooklyn hotel. His
wife and children deserted him when he was converted. The
hotel people named him "Happy Day" because in his little room,
every night, he read his Bible and sang this hymn — "Happy
day, happy day, when Jesus washed my sins away." But one
morning a man who occupied an adjacent apartment said to the
proprietor: "I heard no prayer meeting last night in Happy's
room. He must be sick." They went to his room and found he had
gone to be with the Lord. A newspaper which recorded his
death added: "Always in the early hours of the night when his
devotions would disturb no one, the pious father of a large
family that had forsaken him, sought consolation in solitude and
would let the young men who played billiards downstairs know
that the happy hours of life are those of communion with God."
Is there any name but that of Jesus which can bring such peace
and joy into human experience?

HIS LAST SERMON

I am the good shepherd: the good shepherd giveth
his life for the sheep . . . I . . . know my sheep, and
am known of mine . . . My sheep hear my voice, and
I know them, and they follow me: and I give unto
them eternal life; and they shall never perish, neither
shall any man pluck them out of my hand (John 10:
11, 14, 27, 28).

On a Monday night, the great Scottish preacher, Robert
Murray McCheyne, presided at a meeting of church officers at
St. Peter's and on the way home he performed a marriage. A
little girl ran to him with a beautiful white rose and said: "Will
you put this on your coat?" "O yes, my dear," he said, "but you
must help me." The little child worked to pin the rose in his

buttonhole, where, much faded, it was found after Mr. Mc-Cheyne's funeral. After the rose had been placed on his coat, he had said to the child: "And now will you do something more for me?" "Why, yes," she replied. Then he said: "I want you to listen to the story of the Good Shepherd who gave Himself for the sheep." As he was speaking six other children had gathered around him, pressing as near as they could. So to this little congregation he delivered his last sermon taken from the "Good Shepherd Chapter," the tenth chapter of John. It is said that he told the story as tellingly and as movingly as though he were speaking from his pulpit. We can be sure none of those seven little folk missed the way into the fold of the Good Shepherd.

FAITHFUL WITNESS

> Though I preach the gospel, I have nothing to glory of: for necessity is laid upon me; yea, woe is unto me, if I preach not the gospel! (I Corinthians 9:16). I charge thee therefore before God, and the Lord Jesus Christ, who shall judge the quick and the dead at his appearing and his kingdom; preach the word; be instant in season, out of season (II Timothy 4:1-2).

We never know what will result from faithful witnessing for Christ. In the early ministry of Dr. Lyman Beecher, one of the great American preachers, it was arranged that he preach for a minister whose church was in a remote district. It was midwinter; the day was stormy and cold, and snow lay so deep that he could scarcely find his way. On his arrival, he found the church empty. Nevertheless, he took his seat in the pulpit for it was time to begin the service. After a time just one man came in and sat down. Dr. Beecher arose and conducted the service. The solitary hearer departed. Twenty years later Dr. Beecher was traveling in Ohio when a stranger accosted him. "Do you remember preaching once to one man?" "Yes," said the doctor, "and if you are the man, I have often wished to see you." "That sermon changed my life," said the man. "It made a minister of me and yonder is my church. The converts of your sermon, sir, are all over this state." Little had Dr. Beecher known that his sermon had been greatly used of God.

BETTER HIGHER UP

The Lord is my strength and my shield; my heart trusted in him, and I am helped: therefore my heart greatly rejoiceth; and with my song will I praise him (Psalm 28:7). For our light affliction, which is but for a moment, worketh for us a far more exceeding and eternal weight of glory (II Corinthians 4:17).

We have been told of a bedridden Christian lady whose cheerful spirit amazed all who visited her room. One visitor took with her a wealthy friend who constantly looked on the dark side of things, although she was a professing Christian. She thought it would do this wealthy lady good to see the bedridden saint, so cheerful in her garret room. As they walked up flight after flight of stairs, the wealthy lady drew up her skirts, complaining of the dirt and the darkness of the place. "It's better higher up," said the friend, as they reached the top of each flight. At last they reached the fifth floor and went into the sick-room. There was a neat carpet on the floor and flowering plants were in the window. Singing birds were in cages in the room. There on the bed was the pale, sweet-faced lady. Joy beamed from her face. The rich lady said: "It must be very hard for you to be up here alone this way. I don't see how you stand it." The invalid began to quote precious promises from God's Word, and smilingly added: "You see, I know it's better higher up." *Surely goodness and mercy shall follow me all the days of my life: and I will dwell in the house of the Lord for ever.*

"JOY UNSPEAKABLE"

Ye greatly rejoice, though now for a season, if need be, ye are in heaviness through manifold temptations: that the trial of your faith, being much more precious

> than of gold that perisheth, though it be tried with fire,
> might be found unto praise and honour and glory at
> the appearing of Jesus Christ: whom having not seen,
> ye love; in whom, though now ye see him not, yet
> believing, ye rejoice with joy unspeakable and full of
> glory (I Peter 1:6-8).

A dramatic incident occurred at a wedding in England. The bridegroom, William M. Dyke, had been blinded by an accident when ten years of age. Despite this he had won university honors, also a beautiful bride whom he had never seen. Shortly before his marriage he submitted to an operation and the climax came on the day of his wedding. The bride entered the church, leaning on the arm of her aged father, Admiral Cave. There stood her future husband with his father and the great oculist who was cutting away the last bandage. A beam of rose-colored light from a pane in the church window fell across his face, but he did not seem to see it as with a cry of joy he sprang forward to meet his bride. "At last, at last," he cried, as he gazed for the first time upon her face. What a meeting! Far greater will be the joy of the redeemed as they are presented without blemish in the presence of His glory, seeing the blessed Redeemer face to face. To Him be glory, majesty and power now and evermore.

THE CROSS STANDS

> God forbid that I should glory, save in the cross
> of our Lord Jesus Christ, by whom the world is cru-
> cified unto me, and I unto the world (Galatians 6:14).
> The preaching of the cross is to them that perish fool-
> ishness; but unto us which are saved it is the power of
> God (I Corinthians 1:18).

The author of the hymn "In the Cross of Christ I Glory" was Sir John Bowring. The early Portuguese colonists built at Macao, China, on the crest of a hill on the south coast, a massive cathedral with a splendid approach of stone steps. A violent typhoon nearly wrecked the building; only the front wall remained intact. On the summit of the facade stands a great bronze cross, defying storm and weather. When Sir John Bowring, then governor of Hong Kong, visited Macao in 1825, he was much impressed by that uplifted cross which seemed to defy the ravages of time and storm. The sight inspired him to write the poem:

In the Cross of Christ I glory,
Tow'ring o'er the wrecks of time;
All the light of sacred story
Gathers round its head sublime.

Since that day thousands of visitors have looked upon that same ruin and cross. Some look with indifference, some with curiosity, some with reverence, but few have known that the hymn sung so long by the Church around the world was written by the British governor of Hong Kong as he beheld that same cross which stands today.

BLIND BUT BLESSED

> The Lord maketh poor, and maketh rich: he bring-
> eth low, and lifteth up (I Samuel 2:7). Affliction cometh
> not forth of the dust, neither doth trouble spring out of
> the ground (Job 5:6). It is good for me that I have
> been afflicted; that I might learn thy statutes. I know,
> O Lord, that thy judgments are right (Psalm 119:71,
> 75).

Blind But Blessed was the title of a little booklet by the aged missionary, the Reverend Alex R. Saunders of the China Inland Mission, who is now with the Lord. In 1917 he returned from China to Los Angeles because of failing eyesight. He consulted the finest specialist in the city and was told he would soon be totally blind. What could God mean by permitting this? Mr. and Mrs. Saunders were stopping at the hotel of the Bible Institute. There were days of awful darkness as Mr. Saunders contemplated what was to come. But in their room Mr. and Mrs. Saunders consecrated to God this blindness, that it might redound to His glory. A great victory was won. A few days later Mrs. Saunders led her blind husband to the platform of the Institute that he might plead for volunteers for China. Many then decided to work in China, and twelve graduates returned that fall with the blind missionary, the largest band of recruits since Hudson Taylor led out his pioneers in 1890. The sweet witness of this blind missionary brought hundreds of Chinese to Christ and many missionaries followed to the field because of his consecrated example.

A GOOD MOTHER

Who can find a virtuous woman? for her price is far above rubies. The heart of her husband doth safely trust in her . . . She riseth also while it is yet night, and giveth meat to her household . . . Her candle goeth not out by night . . . She looketh well to the ways of her household, and eateth not the bread of idleness. Her children arise up, and call her blessed . . . (Proverbs 31:10, 11, 15, 18, 27, 28).

There is a well-known painting which pictures the mother of Jesus being led away gently from the terrible scene where her Son was nailed to the Cross. She is broken-hearted, crushed by the sights she has witnessed, yet on her countenance a strange light glows, suggesting faith. The painter has added one touch of his own not suggested in Scripture. In her hand he has placed the thorny crown which once had rested on the brow of Jesus, as though instinctively she lifted the cruel thing from His head. Would not a good mother do this? Yes, it is always Mother who is pulling out the thorns, gently caressing the fevered brow, wiping away the tears, binding up the wounds, whispering words of comfort.

Who is it who wins the crown she wears
When love lays wreaths upon gray hairs,
And joy on wings of softest gleam
Leads home her little ships of dream?
Who it is, though she goes not down
Each day to business in the town,
Still lifts her burdens, toils her share,
Fulfills her trust and meets her care?

SETTING THE SAILS

> The Lord is nigh unto all them that call upon him,
> to all that call upon him in truth (Psalm 145:18). Ye
> shall seek me, and [ye shall] find me, when ye shall
> search for me with all your heart (Jeremiah 29:13).
> Without faith it is impossible to please him: for he
> that cometh to God must believe that he is, and that he
> is a rewarder of them that diligently seek him (He-
> brews 11:6).

When the famous missionary, Hudson Taylor, first went to China, it was in a sailing vessel. Near the Cannibal Islands the ship was becalmed and was slowly drifting shoreward. Savages were eagerly anticipating a feast. The captain went to Mr. Taylor and besought him to pray for the help of God. "I will," said Mr. Taylor, "provided you will set the sails to catch the breeze." The captain did not want to make himself a laughing-stock by unfurling in a dead calm, but Mr. Taylor would not pray until the sails were up. It was done and a little later, while Mr. Taylor was still engaged in prayer, there was a knock at his stateroom door. The captain told him to stop praying. "There's more wind than we can manage," he said. It turned out that they had drifted to within a hundred yards from shore when a strong wind suddenly struck the sails. Mr. Taylor could not have taken such a course had he not been abiding in Christ and ready to obey the leading of the Spirit. "Faith sees the heavenly legions, where doubt sees naught but foes."

PRACTICING HIS PRESENCE

> [The] Lord [is] my strength, and my fortress, and
> my refuge in the day of affliction (Jeremiah 16:19).
> Blessed be God, even the Father of our Lord Jesus Christ,
> the Father of mercies, and the God of all comfort; who
> comforteth us in all our tribulation, that we may be
> able to comfort them which are in any trouble, by the
> comfort wherewith we ourselves are comforted of God
> (II Corinthians 1:3-4).

An aged Scotch Christian lay very ill. His minister came to see him. As the minister took a chair near the bedside, he noticed on the other side of the bed another chair placed at such an angle as to suggest that another visitor had just left it. "I see I am not your first visitor," said the pastor. The man looked up in surprise, and so the minister pointed to the other chair. "Ah," said the sufferer, "I'll tell you about that chair. Years ago I found it impossible to pray. I often fell asleep on my knees. And if I kept awake, my thoughts would wander. I spoke to a minister about it. He told me not to worry, but to sit down and put the chair opposite and think of the Lord Jesus as present in it. 'Talk to Him as you would to a friend face to face,' he said. I have been doing that ever since and how real He has become to me! So now you know why the chair stands like that near my bed!" A week later the man died in the night. He had fallen peacefully into sleep and they found his hand resting on the arm of the chair reserved for the Lord.

GOD AND A BUTTERFLY

I sought the Lord, and he heard me, and delivered me from all my fears. The angel of the Lord encampeth round about them that fear him, and delivereth them. The eyes of the Lord are upon the righteous, and his ears are open unto their cry. The face of the Lord is against them that do evil, to cut off the remembrance of them from the earth (Psalm 34: 4, 7, 15, 16).

A Christian woman's husband, after a protracted illness, was taken from her, leaving her with little to provide for the needs of herself and little daughter. Her husband had been a carpenter and really the only possession of value he left was a large assortment of carpenter's tools. A neighbor who bore no good character, shortly after the funeral, presented a bill for labor which he said was due him. It was not only beyond the widow's power to pay, but she felt certain her husband had paid the bill. It was useless for her to assert the fact for she could find no receipted bill and the man expressed the desire to settle the account by taking all the husband's tools. In great distress the widow went to her room to pray as the man waited for her decision. As she came from her room her little daughter, who had been chasing butterflies, came to report that in chasing one into the garage she had crawled behind a truck causing a pile of papers to fall to the floor from above. It proved to be a packet of receipted bills and the first she inspected was the answer to her problem.

NO PAIN TO SPARE

> O Lord, my strength, and my fortress, and my refuge in the day of affliction (Jeremiah 16:19). Thou hast been a strength to the poor, a strength to the needy in his distress, a refuge from the storm, a shadow from the heat, when the blast of the terrible ones is as a storm against the wall (Isaiah 25:4). I will be glad and rejoice in thy mercy: for thou hast considered my trouble; thou hast known my soul in adversities (Psalm 31:7).

Some of the most beautiful souls of earth have been so afflicted that their bodies bore agonies for years. One such was Dr. Nathaniel Kendrick, one of the founders and the first executive head of what is now Colgate University. He was paralyzed in the prime of life and lay for many years in bed unable to move. It is said that the majesty of his Christian faith made him seem almost divine at times. It is reported that his son once said to him: "Father, I never loved you as I do now. Oh, if I could only bear your pain for you!" But the father replied: "No, my son, I have not one pain to spare. He who allows me to suffer loves me even more than you do and knows just what is best for me. I sometimes think this is the happiest period of my life. His mercies to me are so great." The poet says:

> All Thy griefs by Him are ordered,
> Needful is each one for thee;
> Every tear by Him is counted;
> One too much there cannot be.

And if, whilst they fall so thickly,
Thou canst own His way is right,
Then each bitter tear of anguish
Precious is in Jesus' sight.

NOTHING TO FEAR

Hold thou me up, and I shall be safe: and I will
have respect unto thy statutes continually (Psalm 119:
117). The Lord will perfect that which concerneth me:
thy mercy, O Lord, endureth for ever: forsake not the
works of thine own hands (Psalm 138:8). The Lord
shall preserve thee from all evil: he shall preserve thy
soul (Psalm 121:7).

A party of American tourists was spending some days in
the mountain regions of Scotland. Multitudes risk their lives
in these places to scale heights or descend precipitous slopes. This
party was studying rock formations and flowers. An enthusiastic
botanist saw far below, on a ledge of rocks, some rare flowers
which he was very eager to obtain. No one in the party would
venture to descend. Near by was a father and son with their
dogs guarding sheep. The boy was offered a liberal reward if he
would consent to have a strong rope tied around his body and
be lowered to pluck the flowers. The father gave his consent,
but the boy, although an experienced mountain climber, hesitated to accept the liberal offer. The tourists tried to show him
the strength of the rope, strong enough to hold a dozen men.
The boy's fear was made apparent when he looked at his stalwart father and said: "I'll go if my father will hold the rope."
With Omnipotence upholding us, there can be no duty too dangerous for any child of God. When God's strong arm sustains
us, we have nothing to dread.

A VICTORY WON

Ye have heard that it hath been said, An eye for
an eye, and a tooth for a tooth: but I say unto you, That
ye resist not evil: but whosoever shall smite thee on

> thy right cheek, turn to him the other also (Matthew
> 5:38-39). Recompense to no man evil for evil . . .
> Avenge not yourselves, but rather give place unto wrath:
> for it is written, Vengeance is mine; I will repay, saith
> the Lord (Romans 12:17, 19).

One evening, Hudson Taylor, the missionary, dressed in his Chinese costume, went to the river and intended to cross. He hailed the Chinese boatman from the other side and stood waiting. Presently a richly-dressed Chinaman came down and also stood waiting. When the boat drew near, this man not seeing that Mr. Taylor was a foreigner, took his fist and struck him a blow on the head, knocking him into the mud. Mr. Taylor said he was tempted to strike back but God stopped him. When the boat came up, the Chinaman went forward to get in, but the boatman said: "No, I came at the call of that foreigner, not you." When the Chinaman realized that Mr. Taylor was a foreigner, he said to him: "What! You a foreigner and you did not strike back?" Mr. Taylor stepped into the boat saying: "I've hired this boat. Get in and I will take you to the ship where you are going." On the way out Mr. Taylor poured into his ears the Gospel story. He left the man with tears of repentance running down his face, professing to accept Christ. Thus does God honor and use one who disregards personal affronts, leaving his case in the hands of his Father in heaven.

THE WISE SHEPHERD

> My son, despise not thou the chastening of the
> Lord, nor faint when thou art rebuked of him: for
> whom the Lord loveth he chasteneth, and scourgeth
> every son whom he receiveth. If ye endure chastening,
> God dealeth with you as with sons; for what son is he
> whom the father chasteneth not? (Hebrews 12:5-7).

Mr. McConkey told of a lady summering in Switzerland who went for a stroll and came to a shepherd's fold. She looked in at the door. There sat the shepherd and near by on a pile of straw lay a sheep seemingly in suffering. Asking what was the trouble, she was told that the lamb's leg was broken. The shepherd said he himself had broken it. It was a most wayward animal and would not follow nor obey and misled the others. He had had experience with sheep of this kind, and so he broke one of its legs. The first day he took it food, it tried to bite him. He let it lie for a couple of days and then went back to it. It not only took the food but licked his hand, showing every sign of submission and affection. He said that when it was well it would be the model sheep of the flock. It had learned obedience through suffering. Many times out of our very agony of heart the God of love seeks to bring into our lives the supremest blessing that can enrich and glorify our lives — the blessing of a human will yielded to the will of God. Scripture assures God's children that afflictions are for their profit *that we might be partakers of his holiness* and that we might yield the *peaceable fruit of right-eousness.*

KNOWING THE SHEPHERD

> **The Lord is my shepherd; I shall not want. He maketh me to lie down in green pastures: he leadeth me beside the still waters. He restoreth my soul: he leadeth me in the paths of righteousness for his name's sake. Yea, though I walk through the valley of the shadow of death, I will fear no evil: for thou art with me (Psalm 23:1-4).**

When Dr. J. Wilbur Chapman was traveling through the Scotch highlands, he met a little shepherd boy tending his sheep. "Do you know the Twenty-third Psalm?" he asked the boy. He did not, and so Dr. Chapman gave him the first five words — *The Lord is my shepherd* — and told him to have a word for each finger of his hand. Months later Dr. Chapman traveled through the same section and decided to visit the boy. Not finding him, he inquired at a near-by hut, where he found the lad's mother. She told him the story of how her boy had perished in a fearful blizzard during the winter. He had always treasured the five words of the Psalm and he was specially impressed by the fourth word *my*. He would frequently say the words and, holding onto his fourth finger, would repeat: "My Shepherd, My Shepherd." "When his body was found in the deep snow," said his mother, "his two hands were seen projecting from the snow. He was clasping his fourth finger — and we knew what that meant." Perhaps there are many who repeat the opening words of this Psalm who cannot say from the heart: "Jesus is *my* Shepherd."

THE NEW BODY

> Some man will say, How are the dead raised up? and with what body do they come? . . . God giveth it a body as it hath pleased him, and to every seed his own body . . . Behold, I shew you a mystery; We shall not all sleep, but we shall all be changed, in a moment, in the twinkling of an eye, at the last trump: for the trumpet shall sound, and the dead shall be raised incorruptible, and we shall be changed (I Corinthians 15:35, 38, 51-52).

How can a dead body be resurrected? Part of a body may be buried in one place and part in another! A man may die at sea and be thrown overboard. Fish may eat the remains. Another may be cremated. Is this a problem to the Creator? A man was visiting an eminent chemist who was showing his friend a beautiful silver cup he had received as a prize. Accidentally the cup dropped from his hand into a vat of acid and it melted away like a snowflake. The chemist stepped to a shelf, picked up a small piece of a certain mineral and dropped it into the acid. The silver immediately began to settle to the bottom of the vat where it was collected. "I will send it back to the manufacturers," he said, "and have it recast." If the chemist can do this, cannot our Creator find in His vast laboratory that which can bring together every essential part of the bodies of His redeemed, out of which He shall fashion new bodies in which the living spirit shall dwell again — bodies like Christ's own glorious body?

KNOWING THE SAVIOUR

I {do} count all things but {refuse that I may win Christ}. And be found in him, not having mine own righteousness, which is of the LAW, but that which is through the faith of Christ, the righteousness which is of God by faith: that I may know him, and the power of his resurrection, and the fellowship of his sufferings, being made conformable unto his death (Philippians 3:8-10).

It was the life purpose of a distinguished painter to produce on canvas a picture of the Christ. He worked diligently to record his conception of Christ and, when he had finished the picture, he went outside his studio where several little girls were playing and led one of them into his studio. Asking her to stand before the painting, he said, "Little girl, tell me who that is." She looked intently for a few moments and then said: "It looks like some good man, but I do not know who it is." The artist sat down in deep disappointment. "I fear I don't know Christ," he said. He went to the New Testament and began prayerfully to study Christ. It was not long before he became convicted of sin and saw the need of accepting Jesus Christ, the Lamb of God, as his Saviour. The joy of salvation came into his heart and he began his work anew. When the second picture was finished, he asked the same little girl to look at it. Instantly she began to recite the text: *Suffer the little children to come unto me, and forbid them not.* With tears of joy the artist exclaimed: "Thank God, now I can present Christ so that a little child can recognize Him."

CHILDLIKE FAITH

Come unto me, all ye that labour and are heavy laden, and I will give you rest. Take my yoke upon you, and learn of me; for I am meek and lowly in heart: and ye shall find rest unto your souls. For my yoke is easy, and my burden is light (Matthew 11:28-30). Whosoever will, let him take the water of life freely (Revelation 22:17).

John B. Gough, the evangelist, tells a story about two little boys he once found in a London hospital. Their cots were side by side. One had a fever; the other had been injured by being run over by a heavy wagon. The little fellow who had the fever was very weak. The injured lad said to him: "Say, Willie, I was down to a mission Sunday school and they told me about Jesus, and I believe if you ask Jesus, He will help you. They told us to pray to Him and He would always give us what was best for us." "But suppose I was asleep when Jesus came and couldn't ask Him?" asked the other. "Just hold up your hand, Willie, when you sleep," suggested his little friend, "and I think He'll see you and bless you." Willie thought his arms were too weak, and so Johnny took a pillow from his bed and braced it under one of Willie's arms. The boy went to sleep with his arm upheld. In the morning when the nurse came, she found that Willie had departed from this life. Can we doubt that Jesus saw that little upraised hand as a true expression of faith in Him? Surely He took Willie through the gates of the heavenly city to dwell forever with Him.

ASHAMED BEFORE HIM

> Be ye stedfast, unmoveable, always abounding in the work of the Lord, forasmuch as ye know that your labour is not in vain in the Lord (I Corinthians 15:58). Let us not be weary in well doing: for in due season we shall reap, if we faint not (Galatians 6:9).

Dr. Russell Conwell often told of a trip in the Alps. He came to a shanty owned by a guide who had several valuable dogs used for the purpose of trailing out people who became lost in the woods. One beautiful dog was in its kennel. Dr. Conwell asked to see him but the owner said it was no use trying to get him out of the kennel. He would not come out because of a sense of shame. It seems the dog had been sent out the day before to hunt a party that was missing. All day and all night he had been gone and that morning he had come slinking back with his tail between his legs and looking utterly dejected.

They knew he had failed to locate the lost people. He crept into his kennel and would not come out even for food or drink. The guide tried to coax him out with a piece of meat but it was of no avail. A dumb brute, because of a sense of disappointment through failure to save lives, was heartbroken for days. Dr. Conwell often told the story and remarked about the tragic fact that many Christians seem to have no anxious thought for loved ones and friends whose eternal destiny in heaven was in jeopardy. Alas, many will be *ashamed before him at his coming* (I John 2:28).

"OUT AND OUT" FOR CHRIST

> If thou shalt confess with thy mouth the Lord Jesus, and shalt believe in thine heart that God hath raised him from the dead, thou shalt be saved. For with the heart man believeth unto righteousness; and with the mouth, confession is made unto salvation. For the scripture saith, Whosoever believeth on him shall not be ashamed (Romans 10:9-11).

A young lawyer by the name of McClellan attended an evangelistic service where he heard Christian testimonies of people whose genuineness he could not question. *Such testimony would have to be accepted in any court,* he thought. Then he determined to go forward in personal surrender to Christ. He left the church rejoicing in the experience of salvation. On entering his home he told his wife he had become a Christian and wanted to have a word of prayer with her. "Be quiet," she said. "There are five lawyers waiting in the next room to see you." "Let's go in and have prayer with them," he answered. She tried to steer him into the kitchen, but he said: "I've never had Jesus in my home; I'm not going to take Him into the kitchen the first time." He went in with his visitors, told them of his stand and began to pray in their presence. They all knelt with him, without hesitation and three were converted then and there. Hon. Judge McClellan of the United States Supreme Court never hesitated to show his colors for Christ as long as he lived.

MERCY UNRECOGNIZED

> **When we were yet without strength, in due time Christ died for the ungodly. For scarcely for a righteous man will one die: peradventure for a [beneficent] man some would even dare to die. But God commendeth his love toward us, in that, while we were yet sinners, Christ died for us (Romans 5:6-8).**

A magazine article relating experiences in the Alps Mountains told how large St. Bernard dogs trailed lost persons and saved their lives. The dogs are trained to scratch the snow off and lie down upon the body. Often the heat from the dog's body revives the person, and a flask tied about the dog's neck contains liquor which helps to revive the victim further. One beautiful dog had found its sixty-ninth man. He had stretched his body upon the man, after digging off the snow. The man began to revive and seeing the animal on top of him, thought he was about to be devoured by a wolf. He was able to reach for his dagger and quickly he plunged it into the animal's side. Without a sound the dog crept away to its master's cabin where it bled to death by the doorstep. A few days later mountaineers learned the ful story. The animal's skin was stuffed and his wonderful record was told later to many travelers. Does not one think of God's hold Son who came to earth to save us from our sins and bless us? Yet how many have cruelly stabbed Him, blasphemed His Name and spurned Him! No heart ever loved us as He did. No mind ever planned so much for our welfare as He.

HE CAME DOWN

> **No man hath ascended up to heaven, but he that came down from heaven, even the Son of man which is in heaven . . . God sent not his Son into the world to condemn the world; but that the world through him might be saved. He that believeth on him is not condemned: but he that believeth not is condemned already (John 3:13, 17-18).**

Some years ago a shipwrecked crew was reported as having been cast up on the Rodriguez Islands. They wanted to make the Mauritius, but the common Java fever broke out among them and as they were making for the Mauritius, they were cast on the Rodriguez. The pilot insisted that their sickness was yellow fever, that dismal pestilence so feared by man in those southern seas. There was a French doctor whose business it was to inspect all infected vessels. He entered a small boat and went out a certain distance from the wrecked crew, meanwhile examining the patients through powerful binoculars. In mortal terror, he stood far off to examine them and prescribe for them. But the Lord Jesus did not station Himself on a distant star within hail of this sin-stricken world. He came to earth. He boarded the doomed craft. The black flag of despair was on the earth, but to the amazement of angelic beings, He came to earth to shed His precious blood that a remedy might be provided. He walked among the sinful, healed their leprosy, and left them healing balms for sin-sick souls.

THOUGHTFUL SERVICE

My little children, let us not love in word, neither in tongue; but in deed and in truth (I John 3:18). To do good and to communicate forget not: for with such sacrifices God is well pleased (Hebrews 13:16). We then that are strong ought to bear the infirmities of the weak, and not to please ourselves (Romans 15:1).

Some time ago at Trongate, England, a touching sight was seen. An old lady with a shawl over her head, seemingly very poor, was noticed by a policeman picking up something from the roadway, and hurriedly depositing it in her apron. She continued to do this as though she was finding something of value perhaps dropped by another. The officer, new to his duties, and a bit puffed up with his new authority, went up to the old woman and said rather gruffly: "What is it you're hiding there in your apron? What are you up to? Open up that apron or I'll run you in." The little old lady smilingly opened the apron and there were bits of broken glass, nails and other sharp objects gathered from the path. "Why are you doing that?" asked the officer. "I just pick them up every day," she said shyly, "because so many barefooted children come this way every day and are liable to cut their feet." The big policeman blushed, and putting his big arm around her shoulders, said: "God bless you, lady!" What need there is for Christians who will make it their business to take away the sharp, hurtful things that cause so much sorrow and heartache daily!

DIVINE HARMONIES

> I reckon that the sufferings of this present time are not worthy to be compared with the glory which shall be revealed in us. For the earnest expectation of the creature waiteth for the manifestation of the sons of God. For the creature was made subject to vanity, not willingly, but by reason of him who hath subjected the same in hope (Romans 8:18-20).

A traveler who visited the cathedral at Pisa relates how he stood beneath its wonderful dome and gazed with awe upon its graceful proportions. Suddenly the air was filled with music. The great dome vibrated with harmony. Waves of music swelled like the roll of a great organ, then became soft, far-reaching echoes, melting into stillness in the distance. The harmonies had been produced by the guide who, lingering behind a moment, had softly struck a triple chord. Beneath the magic dome every sound resolves into harmony and no discord can reach the summit of the dome and live. Every voice, footstep, murmur or bustle of the crowd is somehow blended into pleasing notes. If a dome, the work of man's hands, can thus harmonize all discords, can we doubt that under the great dome of God's heaven all can be made to work together for the furtherance of God's redemptive purpose toward all who love Him? Every affliction, tear and grief will be blended into harmony within the overarching dome of divine grace.

MY LORD — AND I

> They went forth, and preached every where, the Lord working with them, and confirming the word (Mark 16:20). It is God which worketh in you both to will and to do of his good pleasure (Philippians 2:13). The God of peace . . . make you perfect in every good work to do his will, working in you that which is well pleasing in his sight, through Jesus Christ; to whom be glory for ever and ever (Hebrews 13:20-21).

Dr. F. B. Meyer tells a beautiful story of a little girl who was staying at a summer hotel. She was of that trying age when small fingers are beginning to find their way about the piano, striking as many wrong notes as right ones, and not particularly sensitive to the anguish such attempts are capable of inflicting on others. A brilliant musician stopped at the hotel. He analyzed the situation and sat down beside the small musician as she thumped out her tunes. He began to accompany her with the most exquisite improvisations. Each note of hers gave him a new motif for chords of surpassing beauty, while many people in the drawing room breathlessly listened. The performance over, the great musician took the child by the hand and introduced her as the one to whom they were indebted for the music. Her efforts had led to his magnificent accompaniment, but his part in the performance had made it memorable. It is the Lord's presence with the Christian that makes the difference. Apart from Him we can do nothing acceptably. If we achieve it is because He works with us and through us. To Him be the glory!

LOVE BEARETH ALL THINGS

> [Love] suffereth long, and is kind; [love] envieth not; [love] vaunteth not itself, is not puffed up, doth not behave itself unseemly, seeketh not her own, is not easily provoked, thinketh no evil; rejoiceth not in iniquity, but rejoiceth in the truth; beareth all things, believeth all things, hopeth all things, endureth all things. [Love] never faileth (I Corinthians 13:4-8).

Stephen Merritt, the great mission worker, who was himself saved from the depths of sin, once gave a supper in his mission to which all outcast and homeless men were invited. After being in the gathering, he took up his hat to go and found that some of the men, in the prankster spirit, had half filled his hat with bacon rinds, pieces of crust and bones. He was furious for a moment and in a towering rage he mounted a chair and delivered a speech. He stormed at the tramps, threatened to call the police and berated them for their ingratitude. Then suddenly there flashed into his mind the words of Scripture: *Love suffereth long, and is kind . . . is not easily provoked . . . beareth all things.* He lived too near to God to be led astray for long. The Holy Spirit rebuked him within, the fit of temper passed and contrition filled his heart. He then and there apologized in all humility, telling them he knew he had grieved his Lord. He then invited them all to another dinner the following night. The jokers at once acknowledged their prank. The next night forty men accepted Christ.

CHRISTIAN RESPONSIBILITY

> Ye shall be witnesses unto me . . . unto the uttermost part of the earth (Acts 1:8). Son of man, I have made thee a watchman . . . therefore hear the word at my mouth, and give them warning from me. When I say unto the wicked, Thou shalt surely die; and thou givest him not warning, nor speakest to warn the wicked [man] . . . to save his life; the same wicked man shall die in his iniquity; but his blood will I require at thine hand (Ezekiel 3:17-18).

S. D. Gordon, in one of his books, tells of a New England minister who, in the course of his pastoral work, was called to conduct the funeral of a young woman who had died very unexpectedly. As he entered the house, he met the leader of the mission where the girl had attended and asked him if Mary had been a Christian. A pained look came over the man's face as he said: "Three weeks ago I had a strange impulse to speak to her about her soul, but I did not, and I do not know." A moment later the girl's Sunday school teacher entered. She was asked the same question. Tears came as she said: "More than once the Spirit seemed to say to me: 'Speak to Mary!' I intended to, but I didn't." The visiting minister then turned to the bereaved mother, long a Christian, feeling sure she would have a better report. She burst into tears and sobbed: "Many times lately I felt I should deal with Mary, but I kept putting it off. I do not know; I do not know!" Alas, so many times loved ones are taken suddenly and unprepared. Why do we not heed the voice of the Spirit of God?

WANDERING SHEEP

> Thus saith the Lord God; Behold, I, even I, will both search my sheep, and seek them out. As a shepherd seeketh out his flock in the day that he is among his sheep that are scattered; so will I seek out my sheep, and will deliver them out of all places where they have been scattered in the cloudy and dark day (Ezekiel 34:11-12).

Agnes M. Winter tells a story related by a friend. During the First World War, several Turkish soldiers attempted to drive away a flock of sheep while their shepherd was sleeping. This incident occurred on a hillside near Jerusalem on a warm afternoon. The shepherd was suddenly aroused and saw his sheep being driven off by the band of Turkish soldiers. This particular shepherd was sympathetic to the British, and, besides, he did not want to lose his sheep. Singlehanded he could not hope to recapture his flock by force. Suddenly he had an idea. Standing on his side of the ravine, he put his hand to his mouth and gave his own peculiar call to gather his sheep. The sheep heard it, listened for a moment, then, hearing his call again, they turned and rushed down one side of the ravine and up the other. It was quite impossible for the Turkish soldiers to stop them, and they could not rush down the ravine in headlong fashion. Soon the shepherd escaped with his sheep to a place of safety before the soldiers had decided what to do. Jesus said: *My sheep hear my voice.* They may be temporarily deceived by fake leaders, but they will come rushing back to *Him.*

TAUGHT OF GOD

Ye have an unction from the Holy One, and ye know all things . . . The anointing which ye have received of him abideth in you, and ye need not that any man teach you (I John 2:20, 27). We have received, not the spirit of the world, but the spirit which is of God; that we might know the things that are freely given to us of God (I Corinthians 2:12).

When Dr. Cortland Myers was the pastor of Tremont Temple in Boston, there were in his congregation two devout colored men. One of them, "Old Black Robert," was one of the most godly men in that great church. He was born in slavery, never saw the inside of a school and learned to read only through great effort. But "Black Robert" knew more about the Bible than any man in Tremont Temple. Why? For years, according to Dr. Myers, he never read the Bible without kneeling and asking the Holy Spirit to be his teacher. Sometimes he read in this way for three and four hours at a stretch. He never went to bed without putting his Bible under his pillow. When they found him dead in a hospital ward, they found the Bible under his curly head. The Holy Spirit taught him the Book. Dr. Myers also told of his godly Hebrew teacher in the seminary. He would come straight to the teaching desk, open his Hebrew Bible, drop his face between the pages and pray: "Lord Jesus, by Thy Spirit, teach us Thy Word." No wonder he taught with such power! He knew his Bible by the same process old Black Robert knew his: he was Spirit taught.

POWER FOR PREACHING

Jacob was left alone; and there wrestled a man with him until the breaking of the day . . . And he said, I will not let thee go, except thou bless me . . . And

Jacob called the name of the place Peniel: for [he said] I have seen God face to face, and my life is preserved (Genesis 32:24, 26, 30).

Not only must the Spirit of God be our true Teacher of the Word, but no man can preach it effectively until he has waited in the presence of the Saviour for power. One Sunday morning a mighty Scotch minister was late in entering the pulpit. The congregation continued to sing but the pulpit remained vacant. At last the sexton was sent to the study to remind him it was past service time. As the sexton rapped softly at the door, he heard the preacher saying: "I will not go except Thou dost go with me." He turned to the deacons to report that the pastor was evidently trying to persuade someone to enter the pulpit with him, but the friend seemed to delay him. More minutes flew by and again the sexton returned to the door, only to report that earnest conversation was taking place within. After some minutes of prayerful singing, the minister stepped into the pulpit. His face was radiant with a heavenly glory. When he read the simple story of the Cross, tears bathed the faces of the people. He never preached with such power. All knew who had entered the pulpit with him when three hundred surrendered to Christ.

A STALK OF CORN

One of his disciples . . . [answered] . . . There is a lad here, which hath five barley loaves, and two small fishes: but what are they among so many? And Jesus took the loaves; and when he had given thanks, he distributed . . . and likewise of the fishes as much as they would (John 6:8, 9, 11).

We are told that in a church tower of a town in Germany there hangs a bell bearing the image of a six-eared stalk of corn, on which is the date October 15, 1729. The first bell hung in this tower was so small that its tones could not be heard at the end of the village. A new bell was needed, but the village was comprised of very poor people and money was not available.

One Sunday the schoolmaster noticed growing out of the church wall a green stalk of corn, the seed of which had been dropped by a passing bird. Suddenly he wondered if this stalk of corn could be made to produce the needed bell. He waited until the corn was ripe and he was able to pluck six ears, which he sowed in his garden. The next year he sowed his entire crop again. Lacking room, he divided with neighbors who continued to sow and reap from this corn for eight years. The money from this corn was taken to the church and kept in the fund for the new bell. At last the bell was bought and its story engraved on the side. We may not be able to do great things or bring large gifts, but if we lay at Jesus' feet the little we have, He will use it, multiply it and bless it.

BLESSING IN CALAMITY

> Behold, happy is the man whom God correcteth: therefore despise not thou the chastening of the Almighty (Job 5:17). It is good for me that I have been afflicted; that I might learn thy statutes . . . I know, O Lord, that thy judgments are right, and that thou in faithfulness hast afflicted me (Psalm 119:71, 75).

A writer in *Putnam's Monthly* relates that a friend of his was owner of a very rare plant which he planted in a large flower pot, placing it close to a basin. It never thrived; in fact, it barely kept alive. Everything was done to revive it, but with no effect. One day the owner went on a vacation and the day he left, a careless boy who was to tend the garden knocked the pot over, breaking the jar, and the plant toppled into the fountain basin. Seeing that the plant had sunk to the bottom of the pool, the boy left it there. When the man returned some weeks later, he noticed one day a new and luxuriant growth of some unknown plant coming out of the water. He then learned what had happened to his plant. Later he learned that it was a water plant and that it had languished by being put in a pot. Even so it has been many times with starving, thirsting souls.

There has come what first appeared to be a calamity, a terrible affliction, a great sorrow. It proved the one thing that was needed to beautify character, to bring out some latent faculty of strength and patience.

A FLOWER'S MESSAGE

The heavens declare the glory of God; and the firmament sheweth his handywork (Psalm 19:1). The invisible things of him from the creation of the world are clearly seen, being understood by the things that are made, even his eternal power and Godhead; so that they are without excuse (Romans 1:20).

When Napoleon was the emperor of France he put a man named Charney in prison as an enemy of his government. He was a learned man and as he walked in the prison yard he looked up to the skies and decided that all things came by chance. One day he saw a tiny plant coming up near the wall, the only green thing in sight. He watched it grow day by day and pondered much about its delicate veins, its perfect design, its beautiful colors. It became his teacher in his loneliness. He made a little frame to support it. On the prison wall he had scribbled: "All things come by chance," but the flower whispered constantly to him: "There is a Creator who made me." The flower so shamed him that he brushed the lying words off the wall, while his heart told him: "He who made all things is God." Then God began to act for him. The daughter of an Italian prisoner who visited the prison noted his love for the flower. The story got to the jailer's wife and finally reached the ears of Empress Josephine. She said: "One who so devoutly tends a little flower cannot be a bad man," and she persuaded the Emperor to set him at liberty. Charney carried his flower home. It had brought God to him and delivered him from prison.

COURAGE TO PRAY

> Be {anxious} for nothing; but in every thing by
> prayer and supplication with thanksgiving let your re-
> quests be made known unto God. And the peace of God,
> which passeth all understanding, shall keep your hearts
> and minds through Christ Jesus (Philippians 4:6-7).
> Pray without ceasing (I Thessalonians 5:17).

A man arose in a church prayer meeting to tell of his Christian experience. He said that he had come from a hospital where
he had gone to have an operation performed on one of his eyes.
In his ward there were about a hundred patients and most of
them apparently were not Christians. As the time came to
retire the first night, he began to wonder what those people
would think about him if he followed his usual custom of
kneeling beside his bed for prayer. He was determined, he
said, even in that public place that he would not neglect his
prayer for himself, his loved ones at home and the people about
him, but he was disturbed by the thought that some might sneer.
"Just then," he said, "I looked across the room and saw a little
boy getting ready to go to bed. The moment he was ready, he
got down on his knees and said his prayers just as he would
have done at home. I tell you," continued the man, "that little
fellow's courage helped me to quit thinking of the people about
me and it gave me courage to join him and let others know that
I was not ashamed of my relation to my Heavenly Father. I
got a great blessing."

WHEN JESUS COMES

> We know that an idol is nothing in the world, and
> that there is none other God but one . . . To us there
> is but one God, the Father, of whom are all things,
> and we in him; and one Lord Jesus Christ, by whom
> are all things, and we by him. Howbeit there is not in
> every man that knowledge (I Corinthians 8:4, 6-7).

She was an old Chinese woman and stood balancing herself
on her tiny bound feet with the aid of a cane. She was listening

to a missionary telling the story of Jesus to a group of women. "That is wonderful," she said to herself, "but the foreigner must be mistaken. I will ask the Chinese woman who is with the missionary if the story is true." "Yes, it is true," said the Chinese woman in answer to her question, "and I will come and see you and tell you more." The next day the Bible woman went to call on her new acquaintance. She spent an hour telling her the Gospel story and about the true God. Finally the old lady said she believed and great joy and peace came into her heart. A few nights later she had a strange dream. A great light fell across the floor of her room and the idols on the shelf began to move. Then a figure whom she took to be Jesus stood in the doorway, and all the idols climbed down from the shelf. "Where are you going?" she asked them. "When Jesus comes, we have to get out," they replied. Then she awoke. When Jesus comes into our hearts the old idols of the world must get out. Our affections must be set on the things above.

LOOKING UNTO HIM

> Surely he hath borne our griefs, and carried our sorrows: yet we did esteem him stricken, smitten of God, and afflicted. But he was wounded for our transgressions, he was bruised for our iniquities: the chastisement of our peace was upon him; and with his stripes we are healed (Isaiah 53:4-5).

Years ago the discovery of the silver mines at Leadville, Colorado, caused intense excitement. Thousands rushed in. A stage was the only conveyance through the dangerous mountains. A party from Denver decided to seek silver, and twenty of them climbed into a rickety old stage and tried to cross the mountains. Breakdowns delayed them and it was dusk when they reached Mosquito Pass and looked down upon the lights of Leadville. The driver dared not go down at night because of the narrowness of the road. The situation was desperate for it was bitter cold. They would freeze if they remained. Finally a tall passenger wearing a white rubber coat volunteered to go down the center of the track ahead of the horses so that he could be sighted by the driver. Hour after hour they wended their way as the man felt his way in the dark. At last they came to the bottom but the leader was cut and bleeding, chilled to the bone. All would have perished had they not followed their leader who risked his life every step of the way. Our Saviour went up the rugged path of Calvary to point the new and living way to glory. His wounds and agony save all who look unto Him.

STANDING WITH GOD

There is one God, and one mediator between God and men, the man Christ Jesus; who gave himself a ransom for all (I Timothy 2:5-6). Who is he that condemneth? It is Christ that died, yea rather, that is risen again, who is even at the right hand of God, who also maketh intercession for us (Romans 8:34). Ye are complete in him (Colossians 2:10).

A poor boy in London, in the days of Baron de Rothschild, the great banker, wanted to become a merchant, but needed assistance. He wrote to Mr. Rothschild but received no reply. He was determined to have an interview with the great man but was not permitted to see him. The young man learned that Rothschild took a walk each morning very early. He decided to hide in the grounds near the mansion, and so he spent the night waiting among the trees. As Rothschild came down the walk, the young man stepped out and introduced himself and briefly told his story. The Baron admired him at once and told him to meet him at his office at eight in the morning. The young man was on hand and was taken by the Baron in his carriage to the London Stock Exchange. On arrival, the Baron entered with his new friend on his arm, and introduced him to various men. The brokers began to inquire about the stranger and vied with one another to get acquainted with him. Before he was through the young man was given a fine offer and became a prosperous businessman because of the standing he seemed to have with Rothschild. The Christian has his standing with God and heaven in the Person of Jesus Christ, God's Son. Through that standing, every need can be met.

OVERCOMING FAITH

> This is the victory that overcometh the world, even our faith. Who is he that overcometh the world, but he that believeth that Jesus is the [Christ]? (I John 5:4-5). Jesus said . . . If thou canst believe, all things are possible to him that believeth (Mark 9:23). According to your faith be it unto you (Matthew 9:29).

A poet and an artist were once examining a painting by Poussin depicting the healing of the two blind men of Jericho. The artist asked: "What seems to you the most remarkable thing in this painting?" The poet replied, "Everything in the painting is excellently portrayed — the form of Christ, the grouping of the individuals, the expression on the faces of the leading characters." The artist seemed to find the most significant feature elsewhere. He said to his friend, pointing to the steps of a house in the corner of the picture: "Do you see that discarded cane lying there?" "Yes, but what does it signify?" asked the other. "Why, on those steps the blind man sat with the cane in his hand, but when he heard Christ had come he was so sure that he would be healed that he let his cane lie there, since he would need it no more, and hastened to the Lord as if he could already see. Is not that a wonderful conception of the confidence of faith?" He was right. Too often we hold on to old canes and crutches and other means of self-help, instead of looking wholly to Jesus, the Divine Helper. True faith drops the old canes at once and leaps toward Him.

A MODERN PAUL

> As many as received him, to them gave he [the privilege of becoming] the sons of God, even to them that believe on his name (John 1:12). He that believeth on him is not condemned: but he that believeth

not is condemned already, because he hath not believed in the name of the only begotten Son of God (John 3:18).

A Methodist preacher in Colorado had a son named Paul. One day Paul was told that if ever he had an opportunity to hear D. L. Moody preach, he must do so. One day Paul heard that Moody was to preach in Denver where he lived. He did his best to get a ticket, but when he reached the building it was filled and the ushers would not admit him. While he stood outside in great disappointment, a chunky man came along and asked him if he wanted to get in. "Yes," said Paul, "but I can't." "Take hold of my coat-tail," said the man, "and hang on." Paul did so and was led to the front. He had been grasping the coat of Moody himself! Moody little dreamed what would happen in the life of that boy twenty-three years later. Paul Rader became a great Christian and as an evangelist himself preached to great multitudes to whom he often repeated the story of how he heard Moody. Paul Rader was called to be the pastor of the church in Chicago which Mr. Moody himself had founded. Here he won hundreds to the Saviour. Later, he himself founded the Rader Tabernacle, Chicago's evangelistic center where untold thousands heard the Gospel message.

LOVE WINS THE DAY

The servant of the Lord must not strive; but be gentle unto all men, apt to teach, patient, in meekness instructing those that oppose themselves; if God peradventure will give them repentance to the acknowledging of the truth; and that they may recover themselves out of the snare of the devil, who are taken captive by him at his will (II Timothy 2:24-26).

H. B. Gibbud, a great soul-winner, tells a story of how victory was won in the case of a woman found in the dives of Mulberry Bend in New York. She was a poor, wretched creature in rags, covered with vermin. Long after midnight she was brought to the mission and Mr. Gibbud called his wife to deal with her.

Mrs. Gibbud arose, dressed and sat beside the sinful woman. She told her of God's love. With a growl like a bear, the woman turned and said: "What do I care about the love of a God in heaven? No one has ever loved me down here." Mrs. Gibbud told her she loved her and longed for her salvation. The woman snapped: "You say you love me. People who love each other show affection. They kiss each other and put their arms around one another. You wouldn't kiss a thing like me." Satan had challenged Mrs. Gibbud at a weak point, but her husband prayed that she would rise to the occasion. Without a moment's hesitation she threw her arms around the woman and kissed her. The poor woman threw herself to the floor, crying to God for mercy. Love had told. She became a wonderful Christian.

LOYALTY TO CHRIST

> Fear none of those things which thou shalt suffer: behold, the devil shall cast some of you into prison, that ye may be tried; and ye shall have tribulation ten days: be thou faithful unto death, and I will give thee a crown of life (Revelation 2:10). Seeing then that we have a great high priest, that is passed into the heavens, Jesus the Son of God, let us hold fast our profession (Hebrews 4:14).

A Roman emperor said to a Greek architect: "Build me a coliseum and if it pleases me I will crown you in the presence of the people and hold a great festival in your honor." The architect did his work magnificently. The day of the opening arrived. The emperor arose amid the shouts of the people and said: "We are here to open this coliseum and to honor its architect. It is a great day for the Roman Empire. To celebrate, bring out the Christians and let them be put to death by the lions for our amusement." The Christians were put in the center of the amphitheatre. The half-starved lions were released from their dens and came leaping forth to rend the Christians limb from limb. The great throng shouted: "Long live the emperor!" Then the Greek architect arose from his seat of honor and motioned for silence, after which he shouted, "I too am a Christian!" He was seized and flung to the wild beasts with the others and was seen tumbling over and over in the dust of the amphitheatre. Could you have done that for Christ before a crowd of people who hated Christ? Do His enemies know that you are a Christian?

PERFECT PEACE

> Let not your heart be troubled: ye believe in God, believe also in me . . . Peace I leave with you, my peace I give unto you: not as the world giveth, give I unto you. Let not your heart be troubled, neither let it be afraid (John 14:1, 27). He is our peace (Ephesians 2:14).

A prize was once offered to the person who painted the best picture depicting peace. There were two that seemed superior. One depicted a summer landscape. A rivulet was noiselessly winding its way through a green meadow. Trees were undisturbed by the faintest wind. The sky was clear. Two cows grazed beneath the shadow of a great oak. A gayly colored butterfly flitted lazily from flower to flower. Birds rested in leafy boughs. This was peace. But the prize was given to the artist who portrayed on his canvas a wild stormy ocean, beating roughly upon the crags of a rocky shore. White-capped waves beat madly against the rocky ledges. The sky was dark and heavy. Lightning blazed across the heavens. But on the side of the rock, sheltered by a little ledge, one could see a pure white sea gull brooding upon her nest. Wild and foaming waves dashed angrily against her rocky retreat, but she felt no fear. Peacefully she viewed it all, knowing she was safe in her sheltered retreat. Christ is the believer's retreat. Seated in the heavenly places in Him, we view all without fear.

INVESTING WITH CHRIST

> Then shall the King say unto them on his right hand, Come, ye blessed of my Father, inherit the kingdom prepared for you from the foundation of the world:

for I was an hungred, and ye gave me meat: I was
thirsty, and ye gave me drink . . . Inasmuch as ye have
done it unto one of the least of these my brethren, ye
have done it unto me (Matthew 25:34, 35, 40).

The wealthy Baron de Rothschild once posed before an artist
as a beggar. While the artist, Ary Scheffer, was painting him,
the financier sat before him in rags and tatters holding a tin cup.
The artist's friend entered, and the baron was so perfectly dis-
guised that he was not recognized. The visitor, thinking he was
really a beggar, gave him a coin. The pretended model put the
coin in his pocket. Ten years later the man who gave it to him
received a letter from de Rothschild containing a bank order for
10,000 francs and the following message: "You one day gave
a coin to Baron de Rothschild in the studio of Ary Scheffer. He
has invested it and today sends you the capital which you en-
trusted to him, together with the compounded interest. A good
action always brings good fortune." The note was signed "Baron
de Rothschild." On receipt of the order the surprised contributor
sought out the baron, a billionaire, who proved to him from
the account books that under his management this small amount
had swelled to this large sum. So Christ is walking through the
world unrecognized today. Blessed are those who give to Him
in the person of His poor brethren or take the Gospel to those,
who have it not. They shall reap treasures untold in heaven.

THE TOUCH OF LOVE

Then were there brought unto him little children,
that he should put his hands on them, and pray: and the
disciples rebuked them. But Jesus said, Suffer little children, and forbid them not, to come unto me: for of such
is the kingdom of heaven. And he laid his hands on them
(Matthew 19:13-15).

Another story about the great preacher, Robert McCheyne
of Scotland, who died when he was a young man, comes
from an American minister who was supplying the pulpit of

that historic church in Dundee. He asked for an old parishioner and finally heard of one aged man nearly a hundred years old who might have known the great preacher. On visiting him, he learned that the old man had known McCheyne well. "Can you recall any of his texts?" he was asked. He could not. "Can you remember anything he said in his sermons?" He could recall nothing. "There is only one thing I can remember about him," said the man — "one thing I can never forget. I was just a boy at the roadside when Mr. McCheyne came along one day. He stopped and came over to the fence where I was standing and he said: 'Jamie, I am going in to see your wee sister. She is dying, and, my boy, I must have you for Jesus. I cannot allow you to go on outside God's kingdom.' He had his hand on my head and I have never forgotten the trembling of his fingers in my hair." The boy gave his heart to Jesus. Perhaps one of the most eloquent gestures the great preacher ever made was when he laid a loving hand on a boy's head. O what good that divine touch would do many a boy!

EYES TO SEE

> **Whosoever shall call upon the name of the Lord shall be saved. How then shall they call on him in whom they have not believed? and how shall they believe in him of whom they have not heard? and how shall they hear without a preacher? (Romans 10:13-14).**

One night in the East End of London a young doctor was turning out the lights of a mission hall in which he was working. He found a ragged boy hiding in a dark corner, where he begged to be allowed to sleep. The doctor took the homeless boy to his own room, fed him and tried to get his story. He learned that the boy was living in a coal bin with a number of other boys. He persuaded the boy to show him where these boys were. They went through narrow alleys and finally came to a hole in the wall of a factory. "Look in there," he said. The doctor struck a match and looked around, crawling into the cellar. Finally he found thirteen boys with only bits of old burlap to protect them from the cold. One lad was clasping to him a four-year-old brother. All were sound asleep. The doctor caught a vision then and there of service for his Lord. He cared for those boys and started the Bernardo Homes for neglected children. At the time of the death of Dr. Bernardo, the newspapers reported that he had taken and surrounded with a Christian atmosphere over 80,000 homeless boys and girls. Hundreds of them became fine Christian citizens. O that we might have eyes to see the need about us! Thousands will drift into a Christless eternity because Christians do not take Christ to them.

DID I DO MY BEST?

> Go ye therefore, and teach all nations, baptizing them in the name of the Father, and of the Son, and of the Holy Ghost: teaching them to observe all things whatsoever I have commanded you: and, lo, I am with you alway, even unto the end of the [age] (Matthew 28:19-20).

Northwestern University at Evanston, Illinois, had for many years a volunteer life-saving crew among its students which became famous. One time the *Lady Elgin*, a crowded passenger steamer, foundered off the shore of Lake Michigan just above Evanston. One of the students of a company on the shore was Edward W. Spencer, a student at Garrett Biblical Institute. He saw a woman clinging to some wreckage far out in the breakers. Throwing off his coat, he swam through the heavy waves and brought her safely to shore. He saw more victims in the water and sixteen times that day he swam out in the fierce waves and brought in seventeen persons. Then he collapsed in delirium of exhaustion. While tossing in his delirium, he cried out, "Did I do my best? Did I do my best?" When his brother tried to quiet him by saying, "You saved seventeen lives," he would reply: "If only I could have saved one more!" Ned Spencer had broken health from that day forward and was unable to take up his chosen work, but he had the consciousness that he had done his best to save human lives. Can we say we have done our best to save lost souls from going into a Christless eternity?

THE SPIRIT'S VOICE

The Spirit also helpeth our infirmities: for we know not what we should pray for as we ought: but the Spirit itself maketh intercession for us with groanings which cannot be uttered. And he that searcheth the hearts knoweth what is the mind of the Spirit, because he maketh intercession for the saints according to the will of God (Romans 8:26-27).

The compiler of this book begs the privilege of relating an incident in his own experience which proves that true prayer is not earth-born. As a member of an evangelistic party we had been assisting in a campaign at Braddock, Pennsylvania. Two of the three weeks had elapsed without results. On a Friday night the evangelist announced that on Saturday night I would conduct a prayer meeting for all who were concerned about souls. The above passage was laid upon my heart and I sought to impress upon those present the thought that at that moment the Spirit sought to lay upon each heart the burden of some soul who should seek Christ on Sunday. I was led to ask for five minutes of silence as each asked God to direct his praying. Many soon began to pray audibly for friends and loved ones by name. The pastor arose and said he was led to ask that all agree to pray ten minutes for these souls before each of the three Sunday services. "I believe," he added, "that God will give us a soul on Sunday for each of those thirty minutes." After prolonged urging a few accepted Christ at the afternoon service. When the evening service closed it was found that the day's total was thirty.

PRAYER FOR THE UNSAVED

I exhort . . . first of all, supplications, prayers, intercessions, and giving of thanks, be made for all men; for kings, and for all that are in authority; that we may

lead a quiet and peaceable life in all godliness and hon-
esty. For this is good and acceptable in the sight of God
our Saviour; who will have all men to be saved, and to
come unto the knowledge of the truth (I Timothy 2:
1-4).

A remarkable visitation of the Spirit, a demonstration of
answer to prayer, is recorded by the Reverend Reuben Emerson
of Wakefield, Massachusetts. An organized band of infidels was
disrupted solely through concerted prayer by a few faithful, praying Christians. The infidel club held regular meetings to promote
their line of thought and attracted many young men of the city.
The situation was alarming. It was felt that argument or force
would be futile, and so the Christians resolved to gain victory
through prayer. They were joined by many praying people who
learned of their gatherings to pray solely for these spreaders of
poison. They claimed the promises and continued to pray. One
day the infidel leader was brought under powerful conviction. He
sought out a Christian and was saved. Then one after another
of the band from week to week came under the same conviction.
Nearly every member was converted. The whole community
acknowledged that it was the work of the Divine Spirit. Not a
word of controversy or rebuke had been said to these men. Like
those at Pentecost, they had asked: *What shall we do?*

INSPIRATION IN SERVICE

The Lord's throne is in heaven: his eyes behold,
his eyelids try, the children of men. The Lord trieth the
righteous: but the wicked and him that loveth violence
his soul hateth . . . For the righteous Lord loveth righteousness; his countenance doth behold the upright
(Psalm 11:4, 5, 7).

The story comes to us of a boy in one of the prep-schools,
an only child, whose mother died when he was young. Between
him and his Christian father a beautiful companionship flour-
ished. The father was blind and his son had to be eyes for him.
Until the boy had to go away to school, the two were together

constantly. The son became one of the best athletes in his school. One spring, just before a final ball game of the season in which the boy was to play an important position, word came that the father was seriously ill and he must come home. There was lamentation throughout the school for it was felt that the game would be lost. The father died, but to the surprise of all, his son returned to school the day before the game and said he intended to play. He played as he had never played before and after the school had won its triumph, the hero player was asked how he had been able in his time of sorrow to return and play so brilliantly. He answered: "Because the thought struck me that my father can now see for the first time—and maybe he would be seeing me play." This consciousness had given him great power. Beneath the eye of our Heavenly Father we are playing life's game. Will we not play better if we remember that His eyes are upon us?

THE LOVE OF MONEY

> The love of money is the root of all evil: which while some coveted after, they have erred from the faith, and pierced themselves through with many sorrows. But thou, O man of God, flee these things; and follow after righteousness, godliness, faith, love, patience, meekness (I Timothy 6:10-11).

Dr. Richard Newton tells the sad story of a sailor who stopped at a small inn at a village in Normandie. He engaged supper and a night's lodging. The landlord and his wife were old and appeared to be poor. The sailor asked them to eat with him and during the meal he inquired concerning their family, asking especially about a son who went to sea when a lad. They supposed he was dead, as nothing had been heard from him for years. At bedtime the landlady showed the sailor to his room. He bade her "Good night," then slipped a little purse of gold into her hand. She showed the purse to her husband and the two were delighted at the sight of it. They surmised that the sailor must have more in his possession. During the night they murdered him in bed and took all his money. Early the next morning two of the lodger's relatives came to inquire about him. They said he had left. "That isn't possible," they said, "for he was your son and he had come home to spend his life with you. He told us he would stay with you one night and see how kind you might be to a stranger." They had murdered their own son because of the cursed love of gold. How many today are ready to sell their souls to the devil for a purse of gold!

MOFFATT'S ANSWERED PRAYER

In my distress I called upon the Lord, and cried unto my God: he heard my voice . . . and my cry came before him, even into his ears (Psalm 18:6). Call upon me in the day of trouble: I will deliver thee, and thou shalt glorify me (Psalm 50:15).

Robert Moffatt tells us that in passing through Africa he stopped at a village and asked for water. The people would not supply it. He offered the three or four remaining buttons on his coat in exchange for a little milk and this also was refused. He continued to plead God's promises. When twilight came, a woman approached from the height above the village. She bore on her head a bundle of wood and carried a vessel of milk. She handed Mr. Moffatt the milk, and without saying a word, laid down her wood and returned to the village. Again she came with a cooking vessel on her head, a leg of mutton in one hand and a jar of water in the other. She prepared a fire and put on the meat. Moffatt asked her repeatedly who she was and why she ministered to his needs. After some time she said: "I love Him whose servant you are and it is my duty to help you in His Name. My heart is full and therefore I cannot speak the joy I feel to see you in this out-of-the-world place." On learning her history, Moffatt found she was the only Christian in the place. When Moffatt asked her how she found spiritual food, she drew from her bosom a copy of the New Testament and said: "This is the oil which makes my lamp burn."

LOST OPPORTUNITY

The Son of man is come to save that which was lost. How think ye? if a man have an hundred sheep, and one of them be gone astray, doth he not leave the ninety and nine, and goeth into the mountains, and seeketh that which is gone astray? And if so be that he find it, verily I say unto you, he rejoiceth more of that sheep, than of the ninety and nine which went not astray (Matthew 18:11-13).

D. L. Moody, the great evangelist, records that on October 8, 1871, he was in front of the largest audience he had ever seen in Chicago. He had just come back from abroad, his first trip, and the text of the sermon was: "What Then Shall I Do with Jesus?" He pleaded with those people and they were urged to decide what they would do with Jesus. As he came to the close of the service, he said: "I want you to take this thought home with you — this unanswered question. Next Sunday night we will gather here before the Cross of Christ and we will answer it." That was on October 8 and it was not more than a few hours until the whole city was ablaze and hundreds lost their lives. Twenty-two years afterward Moody said: Oh, what a mistake I made that night! Never again could I meet that congregation of men and women. I learned a lesson that night I shall never forget. It is my business as a preacher of the Gospel to give the invitation and press men and women for immediate decision." How often, after we have given the truth, we fail to extend the invitation which might bring results!

CONQUERING BITTERNESS

If ye forgive men their trespasses, your heavenly Father will also forgive you: but if ye forgive not men their trespasses, neither will your Father forgive your trespasses (Matthew 6:14-15). Let all bitterness, and wrath, and anger, and clamour, and evil speaking, be put away from you, with all malice (Ephesians 4:31).

Bishop Taylor of Africa relates that he was once having a gathering of native Christians for a communion service. It was a rude communion rail in a forest church and a black man, recently converted, knelt beside two others. Suddenly the bishop saw this man, a former cannibal, looking intently at the man kneeling near him. Then suddenly he arose and fled into the forest. A few minutes later he returned and quietly took his place beside the man from whose presence he had fled. After the communion service Bishop Taylor asked the black man about his strange behavior. He said that he had recognized the man beside him as a man who had slain his father in a battle. Subsequently this man had helped to devour his father at a cannibal feast. He had sworn revenge. Years had passed, during which he had found Christ. At the communion rail the old hatred awoke. He ran into the forest and prayed for power to forgive and to put this hatred out of his heart. On his knees he caught a vision of how Jesus had died to make possible his forgiveness. God gave him the victory and he went back to take communion with the one he had sworn he would destroy. Such is the power of grace in the heart.

TRUE GREATNESS

Whosoever will be great among you, shall be your minister: and whosoever of you will be the chiefest, shall be servant of all. For even the Son of man came not to be ministered unto, but to minister, and to give his life a ransom for many (Mark 10:43-45). Let us not love in word, neither in tongue; but in deed and in truth (I John 3:18).

The ruler of a certain country once decided that his subjects were selfishly intent each upon his own interests, with little regard for helping his fellows. He slipped out one night and placed a stone in the road, too large to be easily pushed aside, but not so large that it could not be moved if one were willing to put forth labor and exertion. The next day the king watched from his windows. Teams drove up. Their owners looked at the stone, and then drove around it. A grenadier in bright uniform lustily berated a populace that kept no better roads, but did not attempt to move it. Travelers came and went, each expressing an opinion that the stone ought to be removed. After many weeks the king sent heralds to summon the people. When they had arrived the king jumped from his horse and removed the stone. Underneath was a box filled with gold, on which was this inscription: "For him who takes the trouble to move this stone." There was no need to point the moral. Each realized that had he been thinking of the good of others he would have reaped a rich personal reward.

PRECIOUS WORDS

> **The fear of the Lord is clean, enduring for ever: the judgments of the Lord are true and righteous altogether. More to be desired are they than gold, yea, than much fine gold: sweeter also than honey and the honeycomb. Moreover by them is thy servant warned: and in keeping of them there is great reward (Psalm 19:9-11).**

Christian Victory magazine tells of an English diamond merchant who was packing gems which he was sending to a trader in India. Each was separately wrapped with the greatest of care. Coming to the last and costliest of all, he used as an outer wrapping the soft India paper torn from an old Bible, the first three chapters of the Gospel of John. A Hindu to whom this precious stone was sent, while unwrapping it, had his attention turned to the sacred pages. The Scripture proved infinitely more precious to him than the diamond which it covered. He soon discovered that it was a message from the Book of Life. He tarried at the words *God so loved the world, that he gave his only begotten Son, that whosoever believeth in him should not perish, but have everlasting life.* Then he began to ask others what these words meant. "Why have I never known this before?" he asked. "Surely this 'Whosoever' means *ME* — this salvation is for *me!*" By simple faith he accepted the words and by the power of the Holy Spirit he was born again. When a European missionary reached that town later, expecting to find no Christians, he found a large group of Indian Christians gathered about this man.

PERVERTED CONCEPTIONS

> I pray not that thou shouldest take them out of the world, but that thou shouldest keep them from the evil. They are not of the world, even as I am not of the world. Sanctify them through thy truth: thy word is truth. As thou hast sent me into the world, even so have I also sent them into the world (John 17:15-18).

In Westmeal, near Antwerp, there is a convent of Trappist monks who represent a strangely perverted conception of Christianity. Thirty-six monks live there under the vow of separation from the world and perpetual silence. They dress in rough sackcloth with ropes about their waists, heads shaven and long beards. They live on bread and sour milk and vegetables and sleep on hard boards. They spend their days in solemn silence. If a visitor speaks to one of them, the monk draws his cowl about his head and moves silently away. Each day they walk in a garden and look into an open grave, ready for the member of the group who will be first to die. This is presumed to be a high ideal of Christian living. These monks suppose that they are illustrating the holiness and beauty of Christianity. But our Lord did not pray that He might have followers of this kind. He did not walk about in silence, but was the sunniest of men, always saying: *Be of good cheer.* He taught His followers that they were not to shut themselves away from men, but go among them daily in the power of His Spirit, witnessing by lip and by life to His saving grace.

GOD'S LEADING

> Praying always with all prayer and supplication in the Spirit, and watching thereunto with all perseverance and supplication for all saints (Ephesians 6:18). If thou

draw out thy soul to the hungry, and satisfy the afflicted
soul; then shall thy light rise in obscurity, and thy darkness be as the noonday: and the Lord shall guide thee
continually . . . and thou shalt be like a watered garden (Isaiah 58:10-11).

Charles H. Spurgeon, who maintained a large orphanage in
London, once went to Bristol to hold meetings in the three
largest Baptist churches. One of his purposes was to try to raise
300 pounds needed immediately for his orphanage. He succeeded
in getting the amount and went to bed on the last night of his
visit thanking God. Then the Spirit seemed to say to him:
"Give the 300 pounds to George Muller. He needs it for *his*
orphanage at once." But what about his own need? It became
more and more clear to Spurgeon that God had spoken and he
must take this money to Muller and expect the Lord to meet
his own need in some other way. The next day he visited
Muller's orphanage where he found the great man on his
knees in earnest prayer with his Bible open before him. Spurgeon
put his hand on his friend's shoulder and said: "George, God
told me to bring you this 300 pounds." "Dear Spurgeon," he answered, "I was just asking the Father for that very sum." The
two men of prayer rejoiced together and Spurgeon went back to
his office in London. On his desk a letter awaited. He opened it
and found a bank draft for 300 guineas — 300 pounds and 300
shillings over.

CHILD'S TALK

Blessed be the Lord, because he hath heard the
voice of my supplications. The Lord is my strength and
my shield; my heart trusted in him, and I am helped:
therefore my heart greatly rejoiceth; and with my song
will I praise him (Psalm 28:6-7). The fool hath said in
his heart, There is no God (Psalm 14:1).

On a large ocean liner a well-known minister spoke one
Sunday morning regarding God's answers to prayer. Among the
audience was a man whose cynical expression plainly showed
lack of sympathy with the speaker's views. At the conclusion

of the service a friend accosted him with the query: "What did you think of the sermon?" The answer was: "Bah, it's mere child's talk!" In the afternoon the minister was asked to speak in the steerage and most of his morning audience followed him. The skeptic found himself alone. Yielding to an impulse, he approached the steward and asked for an orange. "Help yourself," he said, pointing to a large bowl. The skeptic slipped two into his pocket and sauntered toward the outskirts of the minister's crowd. There sat one old woman with upturned face and eyes closed in sleep. Thinking to play a little joke, he gently laid his two oranges in her lap. Later, returning where she was, he found her eating an orange. "Enjoying it, mother?" he asked. "Oh," she responded, "I was so thirsty from seasickness and sat there praying that my Heavenly Father would send me an orange. I dozed off and when I awoke, here were *two* in my lap." The scoffer became a seeker and found the Saviour.

THE POWERFUL WORD

> The word of God is quick, and powerful, and sharper than any twoedged sword, piercing even to the dividing asunder of soul and spirit, and of the joints and marrow, and is a discerner of the thoughts and intents of the heart (Hebrews 4:12). . . the sword of the Spirit, which is the word of God (Ephesians 6:17). Receive [his] instruction, and not silver; and knowledge rather than choice gold (Proverbs 8:10).

Dr. Malan of Geneva was once on a trip to Paris when he conversed with a chap who began to reason with him about Christianity. The doctor answered his every argument with a direct quotation from Scripture. He determined he would not resort to any personal remarks or applications, but would let God's Word be his sole instrument. The skeptic tried to evade his quotations or turn them aside, but Dr. Malan continued to meet him with another. At last the man turned away saying: "Can't you see I don't believe your Bible? What's the use of quoting it to me?" The only reply was a well-chosen verse from the

Bible. Years later Dr. Malan received a letter which read: "You are the man who took the sword of the Spirit and stabbed me through and through. Every time I tried to parry the blade and get you to use your hands instead of the heavenly steel, you simply gave me another stab. You made me feel I was not fighting you but God." At the close Dr. Malan recognized the name of his Paris-bound friend of years before. He had been serving the Master for many years. God's Word is powerful.

TONGUE VICTORY

> The tongue is a little member, and boasteth great things. Behold, how great a matter a little fire kindleth! And the tongue is a fire, a world of iniquity: so is the tongue among our members, that it defileth the whole body, and setteth on fire the course of nature; and it is set on fire of hell (James 3:5-6).

Have you heard the story of the soldier with the biting tongue? He was a brave soldier but he had a mean tongue. The report came that he had been killed in action, and all were glad. Then the next day he appeared. The king noted the gladness of the soldiers on the report of his death and determined to help the fellow if he could. He gave him a bag and told him to bring it unopened to the market place at noon the next day. On the minute, the soldier appeared and the king told him to empty out the contents. He was too good a soldier to ask why. The bag was filled with feathers and the wind blew them in every direction. "Appear here again at the same time tomorrow," the king ordered and obediently the soldier was there. "I want you to gather up those feathers you emptied out yesterday," said the king, "and put them back in this bag." Said the soldier: "It can't be done." Then said the king: "Neither can you recall the cutting words you have spoken about others, no matter how sorry you may be." That soldier later became one of the best loved in his company. How much we need to pray: *Set a watch, O Lord . . . [at] the door of my lips!*

THE UNSHAKABLE FOUNDATION

> Other foundation can no man lay than that is laid, which is Jesus Christ (I Corinthians 3:11). [Ye] are built upon the foundation of the apostles and prophets, Jesus Christ himself being the chief corner stone; in whom all the building fitly framed together groweth unto an holy temple in the Lord: in whom ye also are builded together for an habitation of God through the Spirit (Ephesians 2:20-22).

A bold adventurer once contracted to build a lighthouse on the shores of England. The structure was finished and the builder boastfully declared it would endure the storms and waves. To prove its security, he went into the lighthouse and shouted: "Blow, ye winds; rage, ye waves, and try my work." Night came and with it a terrific storm. When the morning sun arose, spectators gathered on the shore, and, to their amazement, there was no trace of the lighthouse or its builder. Another man, less boastful, then proposed to build another lighthouse on the same point. He dug deep into solid rock, making the foundation secure. The superstructure was firmly anchored to it. When finished, the great light flashed through the darkness and the inscription on its walls could be seen for miles: "Praise the Lord." This lighthouse which still stands is named after its builder — "Eddystone." Jesus said: *Upon this rock [His deity] I will build my church; and the gates of hell shall not prevail against it.* Are you a part of His great lighthouse?

HE LEADETH ME

> Trust in the Lord with all thine heart; and lean not unto thine own understanding. In all thy ways acknowledge him, and he shall direct thy paths (Proverbs 3:5-6). Thou wilt shew me the path of life: in thy presence is fulness of joy; at thy right hand there are pleasures for evermore (Psalm 16:11).

The hymn that has brought light to so many, "He Leadeth Me: O Blessed Thought!" was written without thought that it would be a comfort and a guide to many. Joseph A. Gilmore, a young Baptist preacher of Philadephia, one Wednesday evening gave a prayer-meeting talk on Psalm 23. He was especially impressed with the thought of being led of God and dwelt upon that idea. At the close, he went to the home where he was being entertained and there came to him the words:

> He leadeth me: O blessed thought!
> O words with heavenly comfort fraught!
> Whate'er I do, where'er I be,
> Still 'tis God's hand that leadeth me.

Completing his poem, he handed it to his wife and thought no more about it. Mrs. Gilmore thought much of the words and sent them to the Baptist *Watchman* in which they were printed. Three years later Mr. Gilmore was in Rochester to preach in the Second Baptist Church. He took up a hymnbook to select some hymns. The book opened to "He Leadeth Me." For the first time he discovered that his words had been set to music and published in a hymnbook. One may imagine his thrill as he heard the hymn sung. Yes, "by His own hand He leadeth me."

A HEAVEN-SENT MESSAGE

> My soul cleaveth unto the dust: quicken thou me according to thy word . . . my soul melteth for heaviness: strengthen thou me according unto thy word . . . I have stuck unto thy testimonies: O Lord, put me not to shame . . . Thou art my portion, O Lord: I have said that I would keep thy words (Psalm 119:25, 28, 31, 57).

One Friday afternoon a brokenhearted Christian young woman was in Rosedale Cemetery in Los Angeles, relates Bishop Locke. She was selecting a quiet spot in which on the morrow to lay away the precious remains of her beloved little mother. She was overwhelmed with grief and felt unequal to the task of facing the world with her unutterable loneliness of heart. How could she live without her mother for whom she had tenderly cared throughout more than two years of invalidism? Suddenly, out of the skies, there came and fell at her feet, like a petal blown from a rose, a tiny copy of the Gospel of John. It was dropped from an airplane doing publicity work for Universal Bible Sunday two days later. It came as a direct gift from the God of all sorrowing hearts. As the young woman picked it up, it fell open to the words of John 14:

> Let not your heart be troubled . . . In my Father's house are many mansions: if it were not so, I would have told you. I go to prepare a place for you.

Her tears were dried. She knew her Heavenly Father had spoken and all was well.

FAITHFUL IN OUR PLACE

> He that is faithful in that which is least is faithful also in much: and he that is unjust in the least is unjust also in much (Luke 16:10). Be thou faithful unto death, and I will give thee a crown of life (Revelation 2:10). Let us hold fast the profession of our faith without wavering; (for he is faithful that promised) (Hebrews 10:23).

There was once a poor Irish peasant who could scarcely read, yet he loved to gather his neighbors together in his old barn and try to read the Bible to them and preach the Gospel. In the little company was a young stranger. He was many miles from his cultured home where he had often heard the story of Christ's saving love, but he had never been willing to yield his heart. However, there was something in the presentation of the truth by this stammering backwoods preacher that carried deep conviction to his heart. In that old barn he accepted the Saviour and was born again. It was none other than Augustus Toplady who went forth from the unique sanctuary to become the mighty teacher of the Scriptures and the author of many of our most enduring hymns. The whole Christian world sings his "Rock of Ages." Thousands of hearts have been melted by the hymns of Toplady. Oh, let us be faithful witnesses, however humble our efforts may appear. Little do we know how the Spirit may use our stammering words!

A SINGLE SIN

> Keep thy heart with all diligence; for out of it are the issues of life (Proverbs 4:23). The heart is deceitful above all things, and desperately wicked: who can know it? (Jeremiah 17:9). Know ye not that a little leaven leaveneth the whole lump? (I Corinthians 5:6). How many are mine iniquities and sins? make me to know my transgression and my sin (Job 13:23).

A group of people were walking in a park when one drew attention to a large sycamore tree, decayed to the core. "That fine tree," said he, "was killed by a single worm." Two years previously the tree was as healthy as any in the park, when a woodworm, about three inches long, was observed to be forcing its way under the bark of the trunk. It then caught the eye of a naturalist who was staying there, and he remarked: "Let that worm alone and it will kill that tree." This seemed very improbable, but it was agreed that the black-headed worm should not be disturbed. After a time it was discovered that the worm had tunneled its way a considerable distance under the bark. The next summer the leaves dropped off early and in the succeeding year the tree died and rotted. The hole made by the worm could be seen in the very heart of the once noble trunk. Oh, what a lesson we can learn from that single tree! How many who once promised fair for usefulness in this world have gone down in ruin because they allowed a single sin to have its way until it mastered them!

ROMANS 8:28 PROVEN

> Jesus answered and said unto [them], What I do thou knowest not now; but thou shalt know hereafter (John 13:7). For now we see through a glass, darkly; but then face to face: now I know in part; but then

shall I know even as also I am known (I Corinthians
13:12). Now men see not the bright light which is
in the clouds: but the wind passeth, and cleanseth
them (Job 37:21).

A miner who was a Christian man was often heard to cite
Romans 8:28 when he encountered difficulties or experienced
some misfortune at his work. The miners, most of whom were
rough men of the world, often twitted him about his quotations
whenever he met difficulty. One day they were gathered at
the shaft and were ready to descend. The Christian miner had
laid his dinner pail down by the side of the building, and a
large dog picked up the pail by the handle, as someone had
evidently trained him to do, and ran off with it. At once the
men began their joking about "all things working together for
good," as the owner ran after the dog, trying to get his dinner
pail. Before he returned, the first cage had come up the shaft
and the jeering miners had gone down it. But an accident occurred. A cable snapped and every man in that cage was killed.
That was the cage in which the Christian too would have been,
but for the playfulness of a dog. Often events that seem to be
misfortunes are made to save God's children from great calamities.

HEAVEN'S INHABITANTS

Father, I will that they also, whom thou hast given
me, be with me where I am; that they may behold
my glory (John 17:24). To him that overcometh will
I give to eat of the tree of life, which is in the midst of
the paradise of God (Revelation 2:7). Where I am,
there shall also my servant be (John 12:26).

John Wesley once, in a vision, found himself, as he thought,
at the gates of hell. He knocked and asked who were within.
"Are there any Roman Catholics here?" he asked. "Yes," was
the answer. "Any Church of England people?" and again the
answer was "Yes." "Are there any Presbyterians?" he asked. "Yes,
a great many." "Are there any Wesleyans here?" "Yes, we have
some of those, too," came the answer. Disappointed and dis-

mayed, especially by the last reply, he turned his step upward and at last came to the gates of heaven. Here he repeated the same questions. "Any Wesleyans here?" he anxiously inquired. The answer was "No." And as he named the other denominations, to his dismay, each time the answer was "No." "Then whom do you have here?" he asked in desperation. "We know nothing here of any of those names you have mentioned," said the angel. "They are all *Christians* here — born-again people. Of these we have a great multitude which no man can number, gathered out of all nations and kindreds and peoples and tongues." Let us remember that heaven is a spiritual country for a spiritually-born people. Heaven knows no denominational lines.

"PLUS ULTRA"

As newborn babes, desire the [unadulterated] milk of the word, that ye may grow thereby: if so be ye have tasted that the Lord is gracious (I Peter 2:2-3). Add to your faith virtue; and to virtue knowledge; and to knowledge temperance; and to temperance patience; and to patience godliness; and to godliness brotherly kindness; and to brotherly kindness charity (II Peter 1:5-7).

In days when Spain was the world's leading power, she gave expression to her arrogant pride by an inscription on her coin: *Ne Plus Ultra,* meaning "Nothing Further." It was thought that when one had seen Spain, there was nothing more to see. He had reached earth's limits. But Christopher Columbus sponsored the idea that there was another continent beyond the confines of Spain. His belief led to speech and action. He was considered a fanatic, yet he pressed on amidst all opposition until he discovered the new continent. Then Spain was obliged to change her inscription on her coin to read *Plus Ultra,* which means "More Beyond." There are many Christians who seem to think that because they are saved they have everything needful. Their Bibles are full of directions as to how they may find richer experiences, but they disregard the chart. They neglect the means of grace whereby they might *come in the unity of the faith, and the knowledge of the Son of God, unto a perfect man, unto the measure of the stature of the fulness of Christ* (Ephesians 4:13). Let our motto ever be *Plus Ultra* — "More Beyond."

SPIRITUAL RICHES

Wisdom and knowledge shall be the stability of thy times, and strength of salvation: the fear of the Lord is his treasure (Isaiah 33:6). [There] are given unto us exceeding great and precious promises: that by these ye might be partakers of the divine nature, having escaped the corruption that is in the world through lust (II Peter 1:4).

A Scotch minister tells the story of a poor Scotch woman who went to her pastor in her extremity and told him of the state of poverty in which she found herself. She would have to secure some work in her old age or come to want. He asked her if she had no friend or member of her family who could give her support and she answered that she had a son who was in India in the service of the government. "Does he not write to you?" the pastor asked. "Oh, yes, he often writes," she said, "and he sends the kindest letters and he usually encloses some fancy paper with pictures on the corner. I keep them all in my Bible. But I am too proud to tell him how poor I am and I cannot expect him to send me money." "Would you mind showing me some of those fancy papers he sends you?" asked the pastor. She went to her Bible and took from between the leaves several of the slips. They proved to be Bank of England notes, each for a goodly sum. "Why, you have all kinds of money!" exclaimed the pastor. "You have a Bible full of treasure." How many Christians there are who have untold spiritual riches between the covers of their Bibles, but they do not possess their possessions.

MUCH FROM LITTLE

Abide in me, and I in you. As the branch cannot bear fruit of itself, except it abide in the vine; no more can ye, except ye abide in me . . . [Apart from] me

> ye can do nothing (John 15:4-5). I can do all things
> through Christ which strengtheneth me (Philippians
> 4:13).

A curious bit of history is related concerning the great
violinist Paganini. One night in Paris, where he was to play
before a great audience, as he was tuning his violin, he broke
one of the strings. A wave of disappointment swept over the
audience. Paganini paid no attention to it, but began to play with
the three remaining strings, working his thumb on another string
until that also snapped. Again the audience was nettled, but he
continued to play until a third string snapped and hung down
upon the violinist's arm. The audience plainly was becoming
disgusted, believing he had a poor violin. Quietly stepping to
the front, Paganini said: "Ladies and gentlemen, you now hear
one string and Paganini." He began to bring such wonderful
music out of that one string that the audience leaned forward in
the seats and strained their necks that they might hear it all.
He sat down as the entire house wildly applauded because he
had brought so much out of so little. "One string and Paganini"
— one surrendered soul and God! We may feel we can offer little
through which the Holy Spirit can work, but God does great
things through humble material surrendered to His touch.

TRUE TO CHRIST

> Know ye not that the friendship of the world is
> enmity with God? whosoever therefore will be a friend
> of the world is the enemy of God (James 4:4). Love
> not the world, neither the things that are in the world.
> If any man love the world, the love of the Father is
> not in him . . . The world passeth away, and the lust
> thereof: but he that doeth the will of God abideth for
> ever (I John 2:15, 17).

Dr. J. Wilbur Chapman told of an incident in the life of
Lincoln which suggests a weakness in many lives and an efficient
strength in the lives of a few. He says Mrs. Pomeroy was counted
a member of the President's family circle. One day when he had

grown weary with the affairs of state, he asked her to accompany him to the theater and occupy the President's box at Ford Theater. Mrs. Pomeroy courteously declined. Mr. Lincoln repeated the invitation, but again it was declined. He was a bit irritated and said: "You know it is counted an honor to sit in the President's box. I should like to know why you have refused." As kindly as she could, Mrs. Pomeroy replied: "Mr. President, I am trying to be a consistent Christian and when I became such, I promised my Lord I would go no place where I could not take Him with me or ask His blessing. I do not feel I could do this at the show." Lincoln never again asked her to accompany him to such places, but again and again, when they were driving together on some mission of mercy, he would have the coachman slow down as he would say to her: "Tell me more of the Christ you serve."

HEAVENLY LIGHT

Eye hath not seen, nor ear heard, neither have entered into the heart of man, the things which God hath prepared for them that love him. But God hath revealed them unto us by his Spirit: for the Spirit searcheth all things, yea, the deep things of God . . . Now we have received, not the spirit of the world, but the spirit which is of God; that we might know the things that are freely given to us of God (I Corinthians 2:9, 10, 12).

The astronomer Professor Lewis Swift was at one time in charge of Warner Observatory of Rochester. There was in Rochester a sculptor named Mundy, who was nearly blind. Dr. Swift determined to make him see a star once more. It was winter and magnificent Sirius, brightest of all the fixed stars, was shining in the south. Dr. Swift took Mundy into a dark alley, set up the instrument, trained it on Sirius, and bade the sculptor look. He reported that he could not see a thing. Then Swift observed that a street lamp was burning at the corner of the alley. He suspected that even its feeble light was blurring what was left of his friend's sight. He ran and turned it out to perfect the darkness. Then he had Mundy look again through the telescope. It was a thrilling moment when the eye that so long had seen little of earth and nothing of heaven received the flood of light from above. In rapture he exclaimed: "I see it! I see it!" Before one receives heavenly vision, God often has to deprive him of all earthly lights on which he has depended. When once the mind is set on the things above, there breaks in that light which brings joy eternal.

TEARS OF GRATITUDE

O give thanks unto the Lord; call upon his name: make known his deeds among the people. Remember his marvelous works that he hath done; his wonders, and the judgments of his mouth (Psalm 105:1, 5). Oh that men would praise the Lord for his goodness, and for his wonderful works to the children of men (Psalm 107:15).

In London one of God's great women servants died. Her body was carried into one of the greatest auditoriums of London that the people might pay her honor. A representative of the queen came; lords and ladies passed the casket. Finally the poorer people surged past the casket in hundreds. Toward the last there came a poor woman wearing a little shawl pinned over her head. She carried a baby in her arms and led an older child. When she reached the casket, she put the baby down, released the hand of the older child and bent over the coffin weeping bitterly. She tarried so long that attendants tried to hasten her on. Facing the crowd behind her, she exclaimed, "I walked forty miles and carried my baby that I might see this woman's face. She led my boys to Jesus. They were bound for hell. I have a right to look at her and weep." The people sobbed in sympathy with her. The woman in the casket was Catharine Booth, mother of the Salvation Army. It is well that we ever show gratitude toward those who have made the Saviour known to us and our loved ones. Shall we ever cease to praise Him who has redeemed us by His precious blood?

CLEAN-CUT FOR CHRIST

> Thou hast given a banner to them that fear thee, that it may be displayed because of the truth (Psalm 60:4). Sing unto the Lord, bless his name; shew forth his salvation from day to day. Declare his glory among the heathen, his wonders among all people. Say among the heathen that the Lord reigneth (Psalm 96:2, 3, 10). But it is good to be zealously affected always in a good thing (Galatians 4:18).

Von Zealand, the greatest general of Frederick the Great, was a Christian, but the king was a scoffer. One day the king was making coarse jokes about the Saviour and the whole place was ringing with rude laughter. It was too much for General Von Zealand. He had won many great battles for Prussia and had put the crown on the king's brow. He stood up in a soldierly manner and amidst the hush that followed, shaking his gray head, he said: "Gentlemen, you know I have not feared death. You know I have fought for you in thirty-eight battles and won them all. My hairs are gray. I am an old man. I shall soon have to go into the presence of One greater than any here — the mighty God who saved me from my sin, the Lord Jesus Christ whom you blaspheme. Sirs, I cannot bear to hear my Saviour spoken against. I salute you, sir, as an old man who loves the Saviour and is on the edge of eternity!" Frederick the Great, with trembling voice, said: "General Von Zealand, I beg your pardon; I beg your pardon!" The company dispersed in silence.

OUR SUBSTITUTE

> Christ also hath once suffered for sins, the just for the unjust, that he might bring us to God, being put to death in the flesh, but quickened by the Spirit (I Peter 3:18). Who his own self bare our sins in his own body on the tree, that we, being dead to sins, should live unto righteousness (I Peter 2:24). [He] gave himself for us, that he might redeem us from all iniquity (Titus 2:14).

The history of Persia records this tender incident. Twelve men had been robbed and murdered under the walls of the city. The king resolved that the guilty ones, if found, should be put to death. After a time they were apprehended and their guilt established beyond a doubt. Sentence of death was passed. On the day of execution men and women were in tears because one young man of exceptional promise was among the condemned. They cried, "Can't this young man be pardoned?" But no way was seen. Just before the time came for the execution, the father of this young man went before the king and begged to be allowed to die in the place of his son. "He is young and just betrothed in marriage," he said. "I know he is guilty and deserves it, but will not the law be satisfied if I die in his place?" The king decided to accept the father instead of the son. The son was distracted with grief and begged to be allowed to pay his own penalty, but the father was executed in his place. He went forth free, to live a new kind of life. This is but a faint picture of what our Saviour has done for us. He suffered, the Just for the unjust.

VICTORY THROUGH CHRIST

> The fear of the Lord is a fountain of life, to depart from the snares of death (Proverbs 14:27). There [is] no temptation taken you but such as is common to man: but God is faithful, who will not suffer you to be tempted above that ye are able; but will with the temptation also make a way to escape, that ye may be able to bear it (I Corinthians 10:13).

In a large pottery factory, the foreman, John Foster, was a Christian, and a great temptation came to him while engaged in his work. The president of the concern, who always prepared his formulas in a little private office, was called downstairs and carelessly left his formula book lying open on his desk. Foster had to go into the room for some colors, and he saw lying open before him the priceless formula book. It contained secrets of immense value and he could quickly copy some of them. There were plenty of men who would gladly go into business with him if he could produce a china equal to that made at this celebrated pottery. He could be rich. Many thoughts of what he might accomplish passed through his mind, but soon the struggle ended, for he had looked up. He closed the little book and holding it aloft, said to himself: "Hallelujah! Victory through Christ!" He then sought the president and handed him the book. For many years he stayed with the firm as a humble decorator, but there was real joy in his soul in the knowledge that he was right with God. — *Later became President of the company* *KKK*

HEAVENLY HARMONY

God is able to make all grace abound toward you; that ye, always having all sufficiency in all things, may abound to every good work (II Corinthians 9:8). Able to do exceeding abundantly above all that we ask or think, according to the power that worketh in us (Ephesians 3:20).

Ole Bull, the famous violinist, was making his way at one time through one of the great American forests when he came upon a hut in which dwelt a hermit. He had left his city home because he had been disappointed in business and had become bitter toward all men. For years he had been living alone, his only companion being his violin. Ole Bull stayed in the hut overnight and in the light of the fireplace in the evening, the old hermit sought to entertain his guest by playing for him on his violin the few simple pieces he knew. When he had finished, Ole Bull said: "Do you suppose I could play that instrument?" "It isn't very likely you could do much," said the hermit, "but you can try." The great violinist drew the bow across the strings and instantly the hut was filled with harmony. He played beautiful hymns and "Home, Sweet Home" until the hermit sobbed like a child. He became a changed man. Oh, how many think they have succeeded well, until they begin to realize what music God has put into other lives! What a blessing they could be if they would surrender themselves to Christ, the Master Musician!

MOUNTING EAGLES

> They that wait upon the Lord shall renew their strength; they shall mount up with wings as eagles; they shall run, and not be weary; and they shall walk, and not faint (Isaiah 40:31). Fear thou not; for I am with thee: be not dismayed; for I am thy God: I will strengthen thee; yea, I will help thee; yea, I will uphold thee with the right hand of my righteousness (Isaiah 41:10).

Dr. John McNeal used to tell of one of his friends who had reared an eagle with the chickens about the barnyard, and for this reason the eagle had never used its power of flight, nor seemed to know of its ability to soar in the heavens. The friend decided to move to another part of the country and did not wish to take the eagle with him, and so he set about to teach it the art of flight. He lifted it in his hands and held it for a moment, but it quickly fell to the ground. He threw it above his head but its fall was the more severe. After many trials, in desperation, he put it upon the fence and held it for a moment. The eagle lifted its head and caught one glimpse of the sun. Its eyes had always been turned downward. Suddenly it pushed out one wing, then the other and with a shriek and a bound, it rose from the fence. In another minute it began to soar. Higher and higher it went until lost to sight in the face of the sun. Yes, there are many of us so busy with the things of earth that we become ignorant of the things above and the power we have in Christ to rise into heavenly places of victory.

LOVE DIVINE

> God so loved the world, that he gave his only begotten Son, that whosoever believeth in him should not perish, but have everlasting life. For God sent not his Son into the world to condemn the world; but that the world through him might be saved (John 3:16-17).

A Scotch minister in Glasgow was one Sunday morning trying to illustrate the love of Christ, and told the story of a mother who took her little boy one night and went over one of those Scotch hills. The snow came and she lost her way. Exhausted, she was finally forced to lie down in the snow, after covering the baby with her shawl. The next morning she was found dead. Said the minister, "Her baby was found alive and if that baby grew up, he would be a man over thirty years of age now. If he is still living and thinks of that story of how his mother saved him by stripping herself, I am sure his heart would go out with love to such a mother. He would love her memory and would constantly thank God for what she did. And you, friend, are worse than an ungrateful son if you do not love Jesus Christ who died to save you." Within a few days the minister was called to visit a dying man who had long wallowed in sin. It was the son of the mother of his story. He had wandered into the church that morning and heard the story. He could not get away from the application of the story. On his dying bed he accepted the Christ of Calvary.

ETERNALLY KEPT

> My sheep hear my voice, and I know them, and they follow me: and I give unto them eternal life; and they shall never perish, neither shall any man pluck them out of my hand. My Father, which gave them me, is greater than all; and no man is able to pluck them out of my Father's hand (John 10:27-29).

Two little girls were playing with their dolls in the corner of the nursery in a Christian home. They were singing a song which they had learned in Sunday school:

> Safe in the arms of Jesus,
>   Safe on His gentle breast,
> There by His love o'ershadowed,
>   Sweetly my soul shall rest.

The mother was writing, but stopped occasionally to listen to the little ones talking. "Sister, how do you know you are safe?" asked Nellie, the younger of the two. "Because I am holding onto Jesus with both my hands very tight," said her sister. "But that isn't safe," said Nellie. "Suppose the devil came along and cut your two hands right off!" The older sister looked troubled for a few moments and thought seriously; then her face glowed with joy as she suddenly exclaimed, "I forgot, I forgot! Jesus is holding us with *His* two hands and God's hands also are holding us, and Satan can't cut Jesus off, so we are safe." These were child's words, yet words of true discernment. Many mature Christians miss much of the joy of salvation because they do not realize that they are in the keeping of the Father and the Son.

THE ACHING VOID

> Ye know the grace of our Lord Jesus Christ, that, though he was rich, yet for your sakes he became poor, that ye through his poverty might be rich (II Corinthians 8:9). Whom having not seen, ye love; in whom, though now ye see him not, yet believing, ye rejoice with joy unspeakable and full of glory, (I Peter 1:8).

It is said that when the great violinist, Ole Bull, met John Ericsson for the first time in New York, the musician said to his new-found friend: "Come around and hear me play tonight." The invitation was not accepted, even though given a second and a third time. Finally Mr. Bull said to him, "If you don't come and hear me play, I will come and play for you in the shop." Ericsson replied, "Don't bring your violin into my shop. I don't care for music." But the next day Ole Bull went to the shop and said, "There is something the matter with my violin and I want it fixed." They talked about tone qualities and fibers of wood. Then Mr. Bull said, "I'll show you how it is." He drew the bow across the strings and began to play. The shop was filled with waves of harmony. Men left their benches and came to hear. Ericsson rose from his desk, listening to every note. Finally, with tears streaming down his face, he said, "Keep on. I never knew what was lacking in my life before." The Lord

Jesus is seeking to bring into men's lives that which must fill the aching void if ever it is to be filled. Only through Him can the heart be filled with the harmonies of heaven.

DIVINE PROVISION

I would seek unto God, and unto God would I commit my cause: [who] doeth great things and unsearchable; marvelous things without number: who giveth rain upon the earth, and sendeth waters upon the fields: to set up on high those that be low; that those which mourn may be exalted to safety (Job 5:8-11).

Mr. Spurgeon once went from London into the country to preach. Returning on the train, he found he had lost his ticket. The only other occupant of the compartment of the train noticed him fumbling in his pockets and asked if he had lost something. Mr. Spurgeon told him his ticket was missing and that by a strange coincidence he had neither watch nor money with him. "Yet," he added, "I am not troubled, for I have been on my Lord's business and God has interposed so many times to overcome my difficulties that I feel I will always fall on my feet like the man on the Manx penny." Just then the conductor came through collecting the tickets. He touched his hat to Mr. Spurgeon's companion, who simply said: "All right, William," and the conductor continued on his way. "It's strange," said Mr. Spurgeon, "that he didn't ask for my ticket." Said his companion: "Well, it's just another illustration of what you told me about divine providence watching over you. You see, I am the general manager of the road. No doubt it was divinely arranged that I should be your companion just when I could be of service to you." God never fails to meet every need of His trusting servants.

HONORED OF GOD

By humility and the fear of the Lord are riches, and honour, and life (Proverbs 22:4). Honour shall uphold the humble in spirit (Proverbs 29:23). To this man will I look, even to him that is poor and of a

contrite spirit, and trembleth at my word (Isaiah 66:2).
Let this mind be in you, which was also in Christ
Jesus (Philippians 2:5).

In one of his campaigns, General Sherman decided to
change commanders. General O. O. Howard was promoted to
lead a division which had been under the command of another. Howard participated in the campaign as the head of this
division and then went to Washington to take part in a review.
The night before the veterans were to march down Pennsylvania
Avenue, General Sherman sent for General Howard and said,
"The politicians and friends of the man you succeeded insist
that he shall ride at the head of his old corps. I want you to help
me out." "It's my command," said Howard. "I am entitled to
ride at its head." "I know," said Sherman, "but you are a
Christian and you can take the disappointment." "All right,"
said Howard. "Let him ride at the head." A little later General
Howard received orders to report to Sherman at nine the next
morning. At that time he was told he was to ride beside
General Sherman at the head of the entire army. He protested,
but in vain. "You are under my orders," said Sherman. As a
Christian, he had yielded to another the honor which was his by
right, only to be given a place of higher honor. This is a principle
of God's kingdom. *He that humbleth himself shall be exalted.*
This is the pattern set before us by the Lord of Glory.

DISHONORING GOD

I the Lord thy God am a jealous God . . . the Lord
[thy God] will not hold him guiltless that taketh his
name in vain (Exodus 20:5, 7). Thine, O Lord, is the
greatness, and the power, and the glory, and the victory,
and of majesty: for all that is in the heaven and in the
earth is thine; thine is the kingdom, O Lord, and thou
art exalted as head above all (1 Chronicles 29:11).

A young man had been extremely profane and thought little
of it. After his marriage to a lovely Christian girl, the habit
appeared to him in a different light and he made spasmodic ef-

forts to conquer it. But not until some years had passed did he become victor, when the evil was set before him by a little incident. It was on a Sunday morning and he stood before a mirror shaving. He inflicted a slight cut and true to his fixed habit, he blurted out the single word, "God!" He was not a little chagrined when he saw reflected in the mirror the pretty image of his three-year-old daughter. Hastily laying down her doll, she exclaimed as she looked expectantly about the room: "Is God here?" Blushing and ashamed, the father said: "Why do you ask that?" "I thought He must be 'cause I heard you speak to Him!" said the child. Then, noticing the sober look on his face, the child added: "Call Him again, Daddy. I know He'll come!" The child's trusting words cut to the heart. The father caught her up in his arms and for the first time in his life asked God to forgive him and to make him a real Christian from that time forward.

FAITHFUL WITNESSING

Let him know, that he which converteth the sinner from the error of his way shall save a soul from death, and shall hide a multitude of sins (James 5:20). What man of you, having an hundred sheep, if he lose one of them, doth not leave the ninety and nine in the wilderness, and go after that which is lost, until he find it? (Luke 15:4).

A minister frequently had in his congregation a prominent lawyer who was an infidel. The pastor had long prayed for the salvation of this skeptic, and one Sunday, knowing he was to be present in church, prepared his sermon especially for him. The lawyer was there and listened to the sermon. He went his way apparently unmoved. The next day, however, he went to the pastor and confessed his faith in Jesus Christ. The minister rejoiced and asked what part of his sermon had helped bring him to a decision. "Oh, it was not your sermon at all," said the lawyer. "I did not hear it. I was making a brief all the time you were talking. But at the close of the meeting I saw that old colored lady, Aunt Chloe, trying to get down the slippery steps. I tried to help her down and as I left, she looked into my face and, with tears streaming down her black face, said: 'O Massa Jones, Ah wish you'd take ma dear Jesus!' Those words rang in my ears all day and all night. I got down on my knees in my office this morning and settled everything. I know I've been born again and all my infidelity is gone."

GOD'S GOODNESS

> Jesus . . . said . . . What I do thou knowest not now; but thou shalt know hereafter (John 13:7). Though the Lord give you the bread of adversity, and the water of affliction, yet shall not thy teachers be removed into a corner any more, but thine eyes shall see thy teachers (Isaiah 30:20).

There comes a time when we understand the meaning and love of all God's dealings with us as Christians, however strange and inexplicable they may seem at present. This truth is well illustrated by an old Hebrew story that tells of a rabbi journeying on a mule through a wild country. His only companion was a rooster whose shrill crowing at sunrise awoke him to his devotions. He came to a village at nightfall and sought shelter, but the inhabitants would offer him nothing. Outside the village he found a cave where he prepared to spend the night. He lit his lamp to read a chapter of his Old Testament before retiring, but a gust of wind blew out the light. During the night a wolf killed his rooster and a lion devoured his mule. He passed a sleepless night and early in the morning went to the village to see if he could buy a horse or a mule. To his surprise he found no one alive in the whole town. A band of robbers during the night had plundered the town and killed all the people. "Now I understand my troubles," said the rabbi. "If the people had received me, I would have been killed. Had not my rooster and mule been killed their noise would have revealed my hiding place. God has been good to me."

INFINITE MUSIC

The Word was made flesh, and dwelt among us, (and we beheld his glory, the glory as of the only begotten of the Father,) full of grace and truth . . . And of his fulness have all we received, and grace for grace . . . Grace and truth came by Jesus Christ (John 1: 14, 16, 17).

A soldier, worn out in his country's service, sought to make a living by playing in the streets of Vienna. After a while his hand became feeble and his music was very poor. One day while he sat in great despondency, a man passed who paused and said, "My friend, you are too feeble to play: let me take your violin." He began to play exquisite music. A great crowd gathered and coins poured in until the soldier's hat was full. "Put those coins in your pocket," said the violinist, "and start over again." Again the hat was filled as the violinist played more sweetly than before. Then the hearers began to whisper, "Who is it?" Someone entering the crowd said: "Why, that is Bucher, the famous violinist." Yes, the artist had taken the old soldier's place and borne his burden, played his music, and earned his livelihood. So the Lord Jesus came down, finding us in spiritual poverty. In His grace He took our place, provided for our need, paid our debt and put heavenly music in our hearts. Thank God for the strain of infinite music He has brought to earth!

PRAYER IS ANSWERED

I waited patiently for the Lord; and he inclined unto me, and heard my cry (Psalm 40:1). Verily God hath heard me; he hath attended to the voice of my prayer. Blessed be God, which hath not turned away my prayer, nor his mercy from me (Psalm 66:19-20).

Dr. A. T. Pierson tells how Dr. Adoniram Judson, while laboring as a missionary, felt a strong desire to do something for the salvation of the Jewish people. But his desire seemed not gratified even to his last sickness. He lamented that all his efforts on behalf of the Jews had been a failure. He was departing from the world, saddened by that thought. Then at last a gleam of light thrilled his heart with grateful joy. Mrs. Judson, sitting by his side, read to him a letter from Dr. Hague of Constantinople. It told how, at a meeting of missionaries at Constantinople, Mr. Schauffler stated that a little book had been published in Germany which gave an account of Dr. Judson's life and labors; that it had fallen into the hands of some Jews and had been the means of their conversion. A Jew had translated it for a community of Jews on the borders of the Euxine, and a message had arrived in Constantinople asking that a teacher might be sent to show them the way of life. The answer to all true prayer will come. It may not be in the form we had anticipated, but it will be far-reaching. Judson's prayer was answered long before he died, but the news of it did not reach him until just before his departure.

A QUEEN'S PRAYER

As many as received him, to them gave he power to become the sons of God, even to them that believe on his name (John 1:12). For by grace are ye saved through faith; and that not of yourselves: it is the gift of God: not of works, lest any man should boast (Ephesians 2:8-9).

This true story is told concerning Queen Victoria. There lived on the Osborne House Estate an old lady who was one of the Queen's pensioners, and who had a niece who worked in a business house. One day the niece was at the aunt's cottage for tea and in the afternoon Queen Victoria herself walked in and remained some time chatting with the old lady. After tea, Her Majesty said: "Now I will read a few verses from the fourteenth chapter of John." Then she looked at the young girl and said, "I wonder if you are a Christian, my dear?" The girl replied that she had been christened and confirmed. Without another word the Queen began to pray: "Lord, open the eyes of this dear girl and show her that without a change of heart, she cannot become a true Christian, and show her that no outward observances can in any wise save her soul. This I ask in the Name of the Lord Jesus Christ." Afterward the girl said to her aunt: "I have many times sung, 'God save the Queen,' but I never expected to have her pray God to save me." A short time afterward the young lady was genuinely converted. She became greatly used as a soul-winner for she could never forget the earnestness of her Queen.

THE BIBLE FIRST

> **Blessed are they that keep his testimonies, and that seek him with the whole heart. They also do no iniquity: they walk in his ways . . . O that my ways were directed to keep thy statutes! Then shall I not be ashamed, when I have respect unto all thy commandments (Psalm 119: 2, 3, 5, 6).**

When Matthias W. Baldwin, an engineer, picked up the morning paper to read, his little son climbed on his knee and said: "The Bible first, Daddy; the Bible first!" The busy father thought he did not have time to read the Bible or pray every morning, but he always had time for his morning paper. The voice of his little boy sounded like the voice of God in his heart, but he did not at first heed. Before many weeks those little limbs were still, the childish voice was silent and there was no one to climb upon the father's knee. But God kept the boy's words ringing through the lonely father's heart. Again and again he seemed to hear those piercing words: "The Bible first, Daddy; the Bible first!" In the silent chamber where the body of his little boy lay, Matthias Baldwin gave his heart to Christ and the words of his son became his motto for life. He put the Bible first in his heart, in his home and in his business. God wonderfully blessed him and prospered him and he found great joy in using his money for God. When he died, he left as his monument five churches which he had erected in needy districts.

THE MASTER HAND

> God, who is rich in mercy, for his great love where-
> with he loved us, even when we were dead in sins, hath
> quickened us together with Christ, (by grace ye are
> saved;) and hath raised us up together, and made us sit
> together in heavenly places in Christ Jesus (Ephesians
> 2:4-6).

R. H. Boll tells of an old country inn which boasted a
piano, but it was rickety and distressingly out of tune. Everybody
had banged upon it and the children had abused it with their
fists. Now and then a guest sat down to it and touched it, only
to turn away in disgust. Some laughed at it and exposed its jar-
ring sounds in a spirit of fun. One day there came a master
who knew and loved pianos and music. He touched the keys
and drew back at the weird sounds. Having tuning instruments,
he determined to fix the old piano. He tuned and adjusted, glued
bits of felt on hammers and put in new strings. When he had
finished he ran his fingers over the keys and was satisfied. Then he
sat down and began to play with a masterly hand and as melody
filled the house, young and old gathered around. Those who
had ridiculed the old piano said in wonder, "Who would have
thought it?" So there are sinful souls, embittered and unlovely.
They wait only for the master hand that can redeem them by the
touch of love. It is Jesus Christ who can put divine music into the
hearts of men and make them a praise unto God.

NOTHING IS HID FROM HIM

> Thou God seest me (Genesis 16:13). I the Lord
> search the heart, I try the reins, even to give every man
> according to his ways, and according to the fruit of his
> doings (Jeremiah 17:10). O Lord of hosts, that triest the
> righteous, and seest the reins and the heart . . . unto
> thee have I opened my cause (Jeremiah 20:12).

One day the astronomer, Mitchell, was engaged in making
some observations regarding the sun. As it descended toward

the horizon and began to set, there came into the range of the great telescope the top of a hill about seven miles distant. On the top of that hill was a row of apple trees and in one of them were two boys stealing apples. One was getting the apples and the other was watching to make certain that they were undiscovered. But there sat Professor Mitchell seven miles away with the great eye of his telescope directed fully upon them, seeing every movement they made as plainly as if he had been under the tree with them. Although he could not hear what they were saying, it was evident that they were doing something unlawful. Often men think that because they do not see the eye of God which watches with sleepless vigilance, they are not observed. But not an action, a word or a thought can be concealed from Him. If man with his telescope can penetrate the wide realm of the heavens, cannot God see all that transpires?

GOD AND A SPIDER

If thou shalt indeed obey his voice, and do all that I speak; then I will be an enemy unto thine enemies, and an adversary unto thine adversaries (Exodus 23:22). I would seek unto God, and unto God would I commit my cause: which doeth great things and unsearchable; marvelous things without number (Job 5:8-9).

Our Heavenly Father can spare and protect our lives by anything — even the smallest things. When Claverhouse was seeking to kill the Scottish Covenanters, they were driven to the hills of Scotland to worship. There was an old minister, John Brown, whom Claverhouse had for two years sought to kill. One Sunday morning in one of the highland glens, John Brown was preaching to his flock. Claverhouse and his troops surrounded them. The faithful minister rushed into one of the thirteen caves in the glen. Within two hours the soldiers arrived and began to search the caves. "We have him at last!" said Claverhouse as they went from cave to cave. They came to the last cave, not having found Brown. The minister had been crouching within for two hours. As the soldiers came to the mouth of the cave, they declared, "It's no use to search this one." "Why not?" asked Claverhouse. "Don't you see that spider's web over the mouth of the cave?" they answered. "He could not get in there without breaking that." So they gave up the search. God had sent the spider to do its work after John Brown, His servant, had entered the cave.

THAT WAS YESTERDAY

> Thou shalt forget thy misery, and remember it as waters that pass away (Job 11:16). Weeping may endure for a night, but joy cometh in the morning (Psalm 30:5). Why art thou cast down, O my soul? and why art thou disquieted within me? hope thou in God: for I shall yet praise him, who is the health of my countenance (Psalm 42:11).

The *Moody Monthly* tells that the eminent Dr. Samuel Fallows returned one night to his home from a very stormy session of his church board. It had been the most disappointing meeting he had ever attended. Coming into his drawing room, he dropped into a big chair utterly disconsolate. His wife made every effort to comfort and encourage him but to no avail. He finally retired, apparently whipped. The next morning Mrs. Fallows arose early and slipped down the hall, intending to urge her husband to stay in bed and let her bring up his breakfast. To her surprise she heard him going through his morning exercises, singing a hymn at the same time. "Why, Samuel," she exclaimed, "what about the terrible meeting last night and all the trouble you were in when you came home last night? I thought you would be used up today." As he continued his exercise without pause, he replied, "That was yesterday." Sometimes we allow our yesterdays to steal our todays. *Forgetting those things which are behind,* let us press forward, said the Apostle Paul. No matter how bad the day yesterday, we have twenty-four hours of opportunity today.

THE HIGHER LEVELS

> We glory in tribulations . . . knowing that tribulation worketh patience; and patience, experience; and experience, hope (Romans 5:3-4). Thou hast been a strength to the poor, a strength to the needy in his distress, a refuge from the storm, a shadow from the heat (Isaiah 25:4).

Macmillan points out the remarkable fact that the most brilliant colors are to be seen on the highest mountains in spots which are most exposed to the wildest weather. The brightest lichens and mosses, the loveliest gems of brilliant wild flowers, are formed far up on the bleak, storm-scalped peaks. He says, "One of the richest displays of organic coloring I ever beheld was near the summit of Mount Chenebattaz, ten thousand feet high. The whole face of an extensive rock was covered with a most vivid yellow lichen which shone in the sunshine like the golden battlement of an enchanted castle." Is there not a thought here for the afflicted Christian? The soft airs and delicate showers of pleasant valleys do not always bring out the best that is in him. It may not always be pleasant to climb the heights and share the storms that rage around the Cross of Mount Calvary, but this is what gives brightness and beauty to Christian devotion.

"OUR FATHER IS ON THE DECK"

> I will both lay me down in peace, and sleep: for thou, Lord, only makest me dwell in safety (Psalm 4:8). Let all those that put their trust in thee rejoice: let them ever shout for joy, because thou defendest them: let them also that love thy name be joyful in thee. For thou, Lord, wilt bless the righteous; with favour wilt thou compass him as with a shield (Psalm 5:11-12).

One night when all were quietly asleep, there arose a sudden squall of wind at sea which came sweeping against the side of a ship sailing between Liverpool and New York. The great boat was instantly thrown on her side by the terrific force of the gale, which cracked everything that was movable and awakened the passengers to the consciousness of imminent peril. Everyone on board was alarmed with the exception of one little girl: she was the eight-year-old daughter of the captain. "What's the matter?" asked the child, rubbing her eyes as she was thrown out of bed. Her mother told her of the danger. "But isn't Daddy on deck?" asked the child. She was told that he was at his post. "Then I'm going back to bed," she answered, and crawling back into the rocking bed, in a few minutes she was asleep again.

> Fear not the windy tempests wild,
>   Thy bark they shall not wreck.
> Lie down and sleep, O helpless child —
>   Thy Father's on the deck.

Is there any wiser course in the hour of storm?

IN HIS HANDS

> God is able to make all grace abound toward you; that ye, always having all sufficiency in all things, may abound to every good w o r k (II Corinthians 9:8). We are his workmanship, created in Christ Jesus unto good works, which God hath before ordained that we should walk in them (Ephesians 2:10).

The circumstances surrounding the composition of the beautiful hymn, "Jesus, Tender Shepherd," are touching. The words are:

> Jesus, tender Shepherd, hear me;
>   Bless Thy little lamb tonight;
> Through the darkness be Thou near me,
>   Watch my sleep till morning light.

The authoress, Mrs. Mary Duncan, wrote the hymn for her own little children, less than three years after her marriage, in anticipation of the happy time when she would be able to teach them the simple verses. The time never came, for two or three months later she died of pneumonia at the early age of twenty-five. The verses were not written in vain, however, for thousands of children have lisped them with their evening prayers and many hearts have been touched by the hymn. How often that which has been wrought in devotion to Christ does not find the niche for which it was prepared in our short vision! Nevertheless, in the Master's hand, it is bound to be blessed, and not infrequently He chooses to use it far beyond our fondest dreams. Let us lay our humble contributions at His feet.

THE SNARE OF SATAN

A man is not justified by the works of the law, but by the faith of Jesus Christ, even we have believed in Jesus Christ, that we might be justified by the faith of Christ, and not by the works of the law: for by the works of the law shall no flesh be justified (Galatians 2:16).

A few hours before the death of the great Scottish preacher, John Knox, he awoke from a sleep and was asked the cause of his sighing. He related that he had been suffering a great onslaught of Satan. "Often," said he, "Satan has placed my sins before my eyes and tempted me to despair; often he has endeavored to ensnare me by the allurements of the world, but with these weapons, broken by the sword of the Spirit, he could not prevail. Now he has attacked me in another way. He has labored to persuade my mind that I have merited heaven by the faithful discharge of my ministry. Blessed be God, He has enabled me to quench this fiery dart." The most damning heresy in the world is the notion that somehow man can save himself by his own good works. When Satan comes to the Christian with the suggestion that because of his successful efforts, he has laid up a fund of merits of his own, he is indeed putting forth a subtle snare. It is God who saves us by His grace and it is *God which worketh in you both to will and to do of his good pleasure.*

CLOTHING CHRIST

The King shall say unto them on his right hand, Come, ye blessed of my Father, inherit the kingdom prepared for you from the foundation of the world: for

> I was an hungred, and ye gave me meat: I was thirsty,
> and ye gave me drink: I was a stranger, and ye took
> me in: naked, and ye clothed me: I was sick, and ye
> visited me: I was in prison, and ye came unto me
> (Matthew 25:34-36).

A Russian soldier, one very cold night, kept duty between two sentry depots. A poor workingman, moved with pity, took off his coat and lent it to the soldier to keep him warm. "I'll soon reach home," he said to the soldier, "but you'll be exposed all night to the bitter wind." Some time afterward this working man lay desperately sick and the physician said there was no hope of recovery. As he neared the end, he seemed one night to see a vision. He thought he saw the Saviour. The coat He wore looked strangely familiar. "That looks like my coat," he said to the Master. To his great surprise the Saviour answered: "Do you recall a very cold night when I was on sentry duty and you passed by?" "I remember giving my coat to a soldier," the man answered, "but he did not resemble You." And the Saviour smiled and said: *Inasmuch as ye have done it unto . . . the least of these my brethren, ye have done it unto me.* Christian kindness shall in nowise lose its reward in the life to come.

THROUGH THE VALLEY

> Thou shalt guide me with thy counsel, and after-
> ward receive me to glory (Psalm 73:24). The beggar
> died, and was carried by the angels into Abraham's
> bosom (Luke 16:22). Yea, though I walk through the
> valley of the shadow of death, I will fear no evil: for
> thou art with me; thy rod and thy staff they comfort
> me (Psalm 23:4).

A minister tells of an experience he had when a doctor asked him to go with him to the house of a woman who was very near the moment of death. Reaching the house, the doctor said: "The friends have done all they can do. I will go in first and make her as comfortable as I can. Then I will call you to talk to her." After a time the minister was summoned, and taking the wasted hand of the sinking woman in his, he asked if all was well with her soul. She indicated that she was happy in the Lord. Then she whispered: "I'm going through the valley." "Is there anyone with you in the valley?" the minister asked. She pressed his hand and there came a peaceful smile over her face as she whispered, "Yes." That was her last word. As the physician and minister rode home together the doctor said, "It has been a joy to me to be with you today. I have been brought to realize something as never before." "And what is that?" asked the minister. "I have seen that when friends and loved ones have gone as far as they can go with their Christian dear one," said he, "there is Someone from the other side who takes them up. That woman was not alone as she went through the valley."

THE PULL OF THE WORLD

> Know ye not that the friendship of the world is enmity with God? whosoever therefore will be a friend of the world is the enemy of God (James 4:4). All that is in the world, the lust of the flesh, and the lust of the eyes, and the pride of life, is not of the Father, but is of the world (I John 2:16).

Major James H. Cole, who became an evangelist, related an incident in one of his meetings. A tramp entered the meeting and when, at the close, opportunity was given for testimonies, this man arose and said, "I used to attend this church when I was a boy. My father was an officer here. He used to sit in that pew. There were seven of us boys in our Sunday school class and we liked our teacher. She used to take us to her house Saturday afternoons and we had music and refreshments. Then she began to amuse us by teaching us to play cards. We became more and more interested in the cards. Then we began to neglect her parties and we played cards and smoked cigarettes at other places. Then we began to gamble with the cards and left Sunday school altogether. Two of those boys, both gamblers, have been hanged. Three others are in prison. The sixth and myself would be in jail if the authorities could get us. I have always wished my Sunday school teacher hadn't taught us boys to play cards." An elderly woman, grief stricken, arose and went to the front, where she dropped to her knees. It was the Sunday school teacher.

ALL IS WELL

> Believe on the Lord Jesus Christ, and thou shalt be saved (Acts 16:31). If thou shalt confess with thy mouth the Lord Jesus, and shalt believe in thine heart that God hath raised him from the dead, thou shalt be saved. For with the heart man believeth unto righteousness; and with the mouth confession is made unto salvation (Romans 10:9-10).

Gypsie Hawkins, the English evangelist, relates a story told him by a Christian army officer when he visited Cairo. England at one time had to send an army to quell the uprising in the Sudan. They erected a little temporary hospital on the Sudan desert. Inside the hospital was a Christian soldier, a true servant of God. He was in the last agonies of death and a nurse stood beside his bed. Outside the man on sentry was marching to and fro. Someone came and the sentry challenged him: "Halt! Who goes there?" He demanded the password. It so happened that the password that night was "All is well." The man challenged by the sentry called out, "All is well!" Those words carried by the soft Sudan breeze through the open window of the little hospital fell upon the ears of the dying soldier. His face lit up with the very glory of God as he said, looking into the kindly face of the nurse, "I thank God that, through the precious sacrifice of Calvary, all is well with my soul." As he closed his eyes in death his last whispered words were: "All is well." Are we sure we could meet death with this confidence if the call came today?

UNDYING PRAYERS

> The Lord is nigh unto them that are of a broken heart; and saveth such as be of a contrite spirit (Psalm 34:18). God is our refuge and strength, a very present

help in trouble (Psalm 46:1). My soul, wait thou only
upon God; for my expectation is from him (Psalm
62:5).

A remarkable address was given during the days of the
Second World War by Prince Oscar Bernadotte, brother of the
King of Sweden. The prince is an earnest Christian. He related
that during the First World War, two soldiers, one from each of
the two opposing forces, lay seriously wounded, side by side.
They were able to speak to each other. Said one, "Can you
pray?" "No," the other replied. "I'm not used to doing it." "I'm
not, either," replied the first, "but don't you think you could make
a little prayer?" "I can't," the other replied after a pause. Then
after some silence, the first man, with hands clasped, was heard
to say: "O God, hear my mother's prayers." What a blessing to
have a praying mother! The prince concluded the story with the
words: "I believe that that short, simple prayer rose to the
throne of grace and that the mother's prayers on which it depended were indeed registered in heaven." The remarkable thing
is that young men and women never forget the power and influence of a mother's prayers. In times of acute need, they seem to
cling to those supplications as something no power can hinder.
How much better to know for ourselves the way to the throne of
God through prayer!

LIVINGSTONE'S ANSWER

Christ also hath once suffered for sins, the just for
the unjust, that he might bring us to God, being put to
death in the flesh, but quickened by the Spirit (I Peter
3:18). Ye know that ye were not redeemed with corruptible things, as silver and gold . . . but with the precious blood of Christ, as of a lamb without blemish and
without spot (I Peter 1:18-19).

When David Livingstone, the great missionary, tried to ex-
plain the philosophy of God's plan of salvation to the Africans,
they, hearing the story for the first time, asked him, "Teacher,
how could one man die for the whole human race?" This is

Livingstone's explanation. He dipped his hand into his pocket and brought out two coins, one a common British copper penny, the other a little glittering golden sovereign. He explained that in the country from which he came, the little golden coin which was not so large as the penny and did not weigh as much was actually worth 240 of the copper pennies. The difference in the value was a result of the inherent, intrinsic difference in the metal. So he explained that God's holy, perfect, well-beloved Son was worth a whole world of guilty, lost, condemned sinners. Our hope for eternity is this — and this alone. My sins deserved eternal death, but Jesus took my place, as He did the places of all others who will receive Him, and "upon Another's life, Another's death, I stake my whole eternity." His precious sacrifice cancels all my debt!

THEY UNDERSTOOD NOT

Why dost thou judge thy brother? or why dost thou set at nought thy brother? for we shall all stand before the judgment seat of Christ. For it is written, As I live, saith the Lord, every knee shall bow to me, and every tongue shall confess to God. So then every one of us shall give account of himself to God (Romans 14:10-12).

It was said that the Israelites did not understand Moses. Yet all the time he was true to his people and would have done anything for them. So there are many round about us whose ways and motives we do not understand, and we seriously misjudge them. We find this story from the life of Charles H. Spurgeon which well illustrates this fact. A visitor was at Norwood, their home, one day and observed that young Charles Spurgeon asked his mother for some eggs from their henhouse. Mrs. Spurgeon replied: "Yes, Charles, but you know you have to pay for them." It seemed strange to the visitor that the parents should charge their own son for eggs, and the rumor started that the Spurgeons were stingy and greedy even with their own children. They sold eggs and milk from their private dairy at prevailing prices. Not until after the death of the great preacher was the real explanation made public. Books were found which showed all dairy sales and profits therefrom, all of which had been devoted for years to the maintenance of two elderly widows of Welsh ministers. But the cruel critics understood not.

HAND OVER THE REINS

> Abide in me, and I in you. As the branch cannot bear fruit of itself, except it abide in the vine; no more can ye, except ye abide in me . . . Without me ye can do nothing (John 15:4-5). I can do all things through Christ which strengtheneth me (Philippians 4:13).

Professor Henry Drummond of Glasgow University used to visit some friends in mid-Scotland, spending a large part of his summer holiday with them regularly. On one such occasion he was about to leave after a pleasant visit when they said to him, "There is something we were going to ask you to do for us. You know John, the coachman. We are troubled about him. He has taken to drink and no one has been able to help him. He is now on his last chance with us. Do you think you could help him? Now that you are leaving, perhaps it is too late." But it was not too late for Henry Drummond. When the coachman came for him, Professor Drummond got into the seat beside him. As they rode, he talked about the horses. As they came to a dangerous bend, he asked: "What would happen if these horses ran away with us here?" "It would be fatal," he replied. "But," said Professor Drummond, "if you found they were out of control and you knew that I, sitting beside you, could control them, what would you do?" "I'd give you the reins," he said. "John," said Professor Drummond, "there's a pair of wild horses in you. They'll drag you over the precipice. Why not hand over the reins to Jesus Christ?" As they parted at the train John did just that. The next summer Professor Drummond found John a happy Christian.

THE GOLDEN CROSS

I pray not that thou shouldest take them out of the
world, but that thou shouldest keep them from the evil.
They are not of the world, even as I am not of the
world. Sanctify them through thy truth: thy word is
truth . . . Neither pray I for these alone, but for them
also which shall believe on me through their word (John
17:15-17, 20).

We have heard of the explosive mines that float about in
the sea and act like magnets, so that when a ship passes, the
mine is drawn toward the metal of the ship bottom, and, striking the vessel, the mine explodes. One day a heroic naval engineer took one of these mines apart after it had been washed
ashore, to see how it worked. Soon a way was found to prevent
ships from attracting these mines. It was done by passing around
the hull of the ship a cable charged with an opposite electric
current, which made the vessel as safe as if it were made of wood.
After this had been done, the ship would be marked with a
golden cross to indicate it was safe from magnetic mines. That
golden cross reminds us of another Cross that has broken
the power of sin over the lives of those who have accepted
Jesus Christ. Like ships, we are all made of that which draws
mines of temptation toward us. But those who are in Christ are
prepared against these drifting dangers. They are marked not with
a cross of gold but they are hid behind the Cross of Jesus and
protected by the intercessory prayer of a Redeemer who ever
lives to protect His own.

Ju - Tx. - Ifr atmosphere of Christian

THE MIRACLE OF VICTORY

Love your enemies . . . and pray for them which
despitefully use you, and persecute you (Matthew 5:44).
Let all bitterness . . . be put away from you, with all
malice: and be ye kind one to another, tenderhearted,
forgiving one another, even as God for Christ's sake
hath forgiven you (Ephesians 4:31-32).

The story of Mr. Ling has been related by the Reverend E. Pearce Hayes, a missionary in Loochow, China. It reveals the spirit of loyalty to the precepts of Christ. Mr. Ling, a Chinese Christian, had been paraded through the streets by a Communist mob, assisted by local opponents of Christianity, and led to the execution grounds. A day of terrible persecutions followed, but the man's faith remained unshaken. For some reason, though his enemies had planned to kill him, this man of faith and daring spirit was set free. Some years later a banquet was given on the birthday of the colonel of the regiment and Mr. Ling was one of those present. Next to him was seated a man who was noticeably nervous. Mr. Ling devoted much of his time to trying to make this man at ease, and spoke most kindly to him, but his efforts failed. Soon the uneasy guest excused himself and departed from the banquet hall. Mr. Ling then revealed the fact that this man had been the leader of the parade on the day when the Communists had led him to the execution ground. The natural thing for Mr. Ling to have done would have been to ignore his enemy, but he revealed a miracle of Christian victory, showing the spirit of forgiveness and friendship.

DIVINE LOVE SPURNED

> God so loved the world, that he gave his only begotten Son (John 3:16). [But] ye will not come to me, that ye might have [everlasting] life (John 5:40). He came unto his own, and his own received him not (John 1:11). He is despised and rejected of men; a man of sorrows, and acquainted with grief: and we hid as it were our faces from him; he was despised, and we esteemed him not (Isaiah 53:3).

"I was lying one night in Plymouth Sound aboard my fishing boat," says an old fisherman, "when I heard a splash in the water. I was out of my berth in a minute, for I knew there was a fishing craft not far off, and I suspected that the man was drunk and, in trying to get out of his boat, had fallen overboard. I jumped into my boat and rowed with all my might, praying meanwhile that God would help me to find him. Presently I saw him. Getting hold of his arm, I managed finally to pull him into my boat. Then I took him to his own boat. I worked over him a long time till I knew he was in a safe condition to leave. Next morning he was leaning over the side of his craft when I pulled over to see how he was. 'How are you this morning?' I asked. 'What's that to you?' he asked. 'I was interested,' I answered, 'because I saved your life last night.' He cursed me and called me a liar. My heart was like a thing broken and I pulled away. 'Oh, Jesus,' I said, 'I know now how You feel. This is the way millions are always treating You — You who gave Your life for them.'"

OBSCURE WITNESSES

> Be strong in the grace that is in Christ Jesus. And the things that thou hast heard . . . the same commit thou to faithful men, who shall be able to teach others also. Thou therefore endure hardness, as a good soldier of Jesus Christ (II Timothy 2:1-3). Preach the word; be instant in season, out of season (II Timothy 4:2).

A century and a half ago there died a humble minister, pastor of a small village congregation in Leicestershire, England. He had never attended college and had no degrees. He was merely a faithful village minister. In his congregation was a young cobbler to whom the minister gave special attention, teaching him the Word of God. This young man was later to be renowned as William Carey, one of the greatest missionaries of modern times. That same humble minister had a son, a boy whom he taught faithfully and constantly encouraged. The boy's character and powers were profoundly affected by his father's life. That son was Robert Hall, the mightiest public orator of his day, whose sermons influenced the decisions of statesmen and whose character was as saintly as his preaching was phenomenal. It seemed that the village pastor accomplished little. There were no spectacular revivals, but his faithful witness and godly life had much to do with giving India its Carey and England its Robert Hall. Let those who think they are obscure do their best. God will not leave such witness without fruitage.

THE MELTED MOUNTAIN

Not by works of righteousness which we have done, but according to his mercy he saved us, by the washing of regeneration, and renewing of the Holy Ghost; which he shed on us abundantly through Jesus Christ our Saviour; that being justified by his grace, we should be made heirs according to the hope of eternal life (Titus 3:5-7).

John Williams, a pioneer missionary to the South Sea Islands, has left on record a touching account of the conversion of a native man named "Me." He became blind and at last lay down on his rough bed to die. One morning Mr. Williams called to see him. "Last night," said the old man, "I had a wonderful dream." "Tell me your dream," said the missionary. "I dreamed I was on a long journey to my final home," he said. "Before me I saw a mountain barring my path. I began to climb it but it was very steep and its rough stones cut my feet. I fell back and rolled down to its base exhausted. Again and again I tried, but it was useless. I felt more and more how helpless I was to reach the other side. Then as I looked up I saw a drop of blood fall from the sky to the mountain peak. At once the mountain began to melt away and soon it was gone. Hope and joy filled my heart and I started on my journey — but then my dream ended. And now I know the mountain was my sins which blocked the way and it was Christ's precious blood that opened the way to heaven for me."

THE FACE DIVINE

Wherefore seeing we also are compassed about with so great a cloud of witnesses, let us lay aside every weight, and the sin which doth so easily beset us, and let us run with patience the race that is set before

> us, looking unto Jesus the author and finisher of our
> faith; who for the joy that was set before him endured
> the cross, despising the shame, and is set down at the
> right hand of the throne of God (Hebrews 12:1-2).

A famous painter of olden times made a rule that none of
those who came to learn in his studio should be allowed to paint
the face of our Lord unless he were pure in heart and life. One
day a young man came who was suspected of leading a wild life.
The artist told him of his rule and gave him a head of Judas
Iscariot to copy. He tried for some time to copy it but the face
repelled him so that he came to loathe it. At last he said de-
spairingly: "Master, I cannot reproduce this. Only give me the
face of Christ and I will do my best." The artist complied with
his request. As the pupil studied the sweetness and moral beauty
of the face divine, its mute appeal awakened in his heart a desire
to know Him. Then and there he came to hate his old life and
to love goodness and purity for the sake of Him who gave His
life for the world. It is only by *looking unto Jesus* and contemplat-
ing the love of God revealed in Him that we can see vice in its
true colors and come to know the joy of walking in His steps.

THE LOST PAINTING

> Whom he did foreknow, he also did predestinate
> to be conformed to the image of his Son (Romans 8:29).
> Be not conformed to this world: but be ye transformed
> by the renewing of your mind, that ye may prove what is
> that good, and acceptable, and perfect, will of God
> (Romans 12:2). Let this mind be in you, which was
> also in Christ Jesus (Philippians 2:5).

There is an interesting story concerning the portrait of Dante
which was painted upon the walls of the Bargello at Florence,
Italy. Dr. Henry Van Dyke tells us that for many years it was
supposed that this valuable picture had utterly perished. There
were many reports concerning it, but no one living had seen it.
Presently an artist came who was determined to find the original.
He went into the old palace where tradition said it had been

painted. The room in question was used at the time for storing lumber and straw. The walls were covered with whitewash and dirt. The artist had heaps of rubbish carried away. Patiently and carefully he removed the whitewash from the walls. Lines and colors long hidden began to appear. He knew he had found the painting. At last the grave, lofty, noble face of the great poet looked out upon the world of light again. Dr. Van Dyke says that was not half so wonderful as the work Christ came to do in the heart of man, to restore the forgotten image of God. He comes to us and touches us with the faith that the divine image can be restored. Will we submit to the cleansing work of the Holy Spirit?

LOVE CONFESSED

> Jesus saith to Simon Peter, Simon, son of Jonas, lovest thou me more than these? He saith unto him, Yea, Lord; thou knowest that I love thee. He saith unto him, Feed my lambs. He saith to him again the second time, Simon, son of Jonas, lovest thou me? . . . [and] . . . the third time . . . Lovest thou me? And he said . . . thou knowest that I love thee. Jesus saith unto him, Feed my sheep (John 21:15-17).

A widower had an only child, a little girl, who was deaf and dumb. He loved her intensely and between them they had learned a kind of sign language. Finally the father had to leave home and go abroad on business. Before doing so, he took his daughter to an institution where deaf children were taught the lip language. On his return, he went immediately to see her. She had been told that he was coming and was watching for him at a window overlooking the drive which led to the building. As soon as he appeared at the gate, she ran down the stairs and through the hall door to greet him. Climbing into his outstretched arms, she put her lips against his ear and said: "Daddy, I love you." The man was overcome with emotion and sobbed for joy as he pressed his child to his heart. It hardly seemed possible that at last he had heard her speak these words. Does not our Heavenly Father derive a special joy — and does not our Lord —

in hearing from our lips an avowal of our love? If we love Jesus, should we not tell Him so often, even though we are conscious that our love should be far deeper?

KING OF KINGS

> I beheld, and I heard the voice of many angels round about the throne and the [creatures] and the elders: and the number of them was ten thousand times ten thousand, and thousands of thousands; saying with a loud voice, Worthy is the Lamb that was slain to receive power, and riches, and wisdom, and strength, and honour, and glory, and blessing (Revelation 5:11-12).

It is recorded of Queen Victoria, that in the year of her coronation she attended a public performance of Handel's oratorio, *The Messiah*. She had been instructed by her court advisers that whereas the audience would rise and remain standing when the "Hallelujah Chorus" was sung, it was the royal prerogative to remain seated. So when the chorus began, those in the vast audience rose to their feet. At first there was a struggle in the Queen's mind between the wish to observe court etiquette and the instincts of her heart, which moved her to honor the Lord she loved. When the choir sang the inspiring passage *King of kings, and Lord of lords,* the Queen rose to her feet and stood in the royal box, thus bearing witness to Christ her Lord. It was only what might have been expected from devout Queen Victoria. There are times when the pent-up floods of emotion of every spiritual nature must burst open the sluice gates or overflow the barriers of social customs and human restraints. Let us on every possible occasion give honor to Him who has redeemed us by His precious blood, not fearing to confess His Name.

Printed in the United States of America